THE HURRICANE OF 1938

Memories of the Storm of the Century

by Chris Wisniewski

Saving Stories

· Personal Historian ·
Researcher · Book Designer

Revised paperback edition, 2022.
ISBN 978-0-9910772-5-0

First printed in hardcover, 2013.
[ISBN 978-0-9910772-0-5]

Compiled and edited by Chris Wisniewski.
Layout and design by Saving Stories.
Saving your memories and personal history.
www.saving-stories.com
978-590-1084

Front cover photograph by Edward & Mary Carlson.
Back cover photograph by Ada R. Chase from the collection of Diane A. Norman.

The Path of the Hurricane

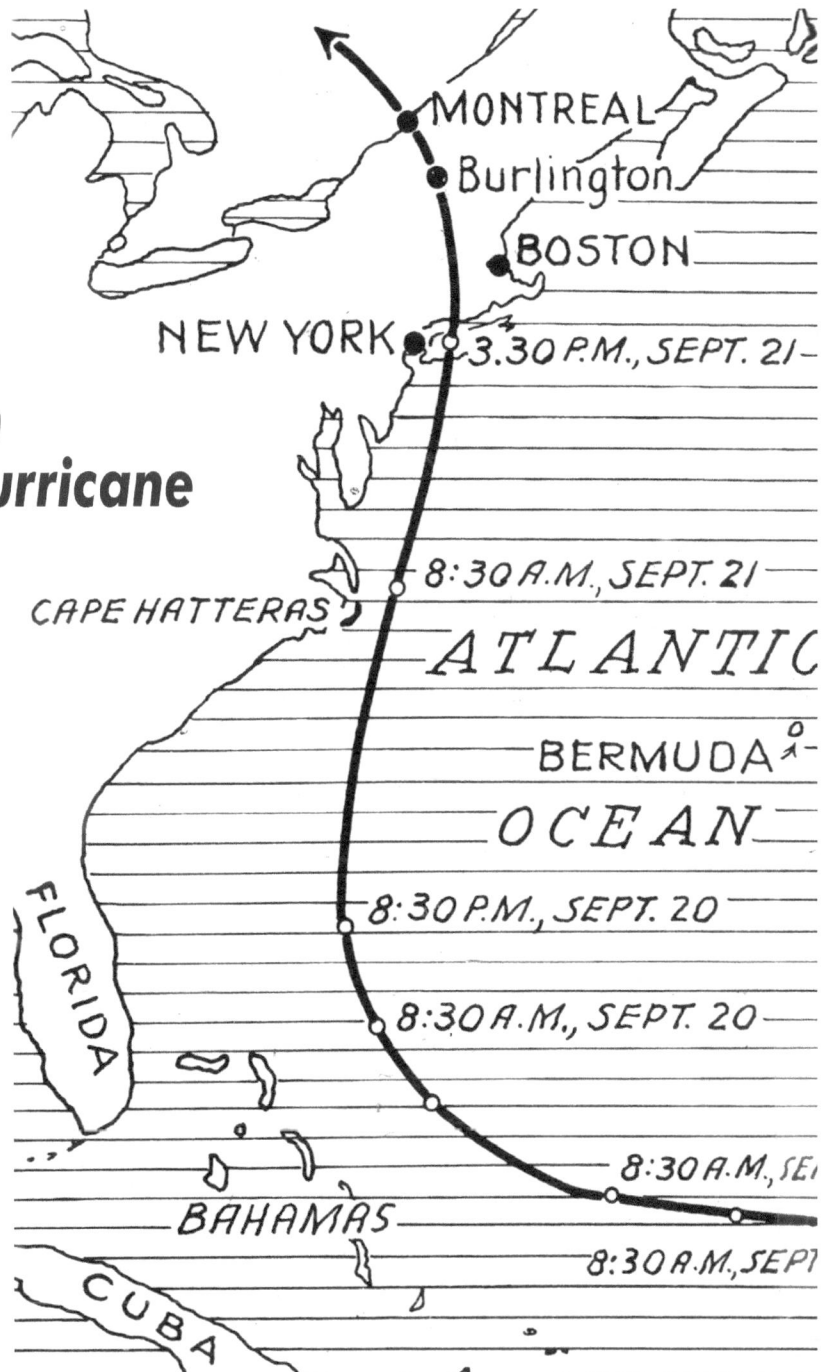

MONTREAL
Burlington
BOSTON
NEW YORK — 3.30 P.M., SEPT. 21
8:30 A.M., SEPT. 21
CAPE HATTERAS
ATLANTIC
BERMUDA
OCEAN
8:30 P.M., SEPT. 20
8:30 A.M., SEPT. 20
FLORIDA
8:30 A.M., SE
BAHAMAS
8:30 A.M., SEPT
CUBA
8:30 A.M., SEPT

Map from "An Album of Pictures of the New England Hurricane and Floods of September, 1938"
by Leslie H. Tyler.

For Ed and Betty—
the first to tell me stories of when the wind blew.

In 2013, I was asked by *The Norwich Bulletin* to partner with them on a book to commemorate the 75th anniversary of the 1938 Hurricane. I had long been intrigued by the tales of the storm that I had heard from my parents, even though their stories had seemed rather far fetched and exaggerated, so I was excited to speak with others to hear more of what had actually happened.

The Bulletin put out the word that I was looking for people to interview about their memories of the hurricane and for photographs taken during the storm or in the days afterward. Since the storm occurred 75 years ago, I was unsure what the response would be. I was pleased and surprised to have more than 65 people contact me with memories of that day and still more people who were willing to share photographs that they or their parents had taken of the damage caused by the storm.

The interviews were all conducted in a relatively short period of time. The stories covered just the day of the storm, September 21, 1938, and the days immediately after, and almost all of the people I spoke to had lived in and around Norwich, Connecticut, in 1938. As a result I found that many of their stories began to overlap. One person would tell me they had walked by a school just after one of its walls fell down, then another person would tell me they had been standing in the doorway of that school as the wall fell. One person told me they had to get across a bridge that had been flooded out and some people had set up a pulley system to pull a small boat back and forth to let people safely cross the river. Then another person told me her brothers had been the ones to swim across the river with the rope to pull the boats and that they had almost been washed away. The stories, told together, give a multi-sided view of the events of the day. They also offer interesting details of life in southeastern New England in the late 1930s.

It was fascinating listening to these memories, and I soon realized the stories I had heard years ago were not at all exaggerated. The interviews that stuck with me the most were ones where I watched as 80 or 90-year-old men and women reverted back to young children, either terrified or fascinated with the storm. Their memories were still so raw and the events they witnessed so extreme that, even after 75 years, the intensity of their emotions came through in the telling.

I am so grateful to all the people who stepped up and offered their memories or photographs to document this storm. They made me appreciate the history of places I had known well, but now understand better. And now, ten years after the first printing of this book, I am even more grateful to have captured these memories when I did. It was a wonderful opportunity to save these stories.

— Chris Wisniewski
April, 2022

The Palace Theater on Rose Place in Norwich, Conn. The railroad trestle bridge is in the background.
— *photograph from the collection of Robert Rousseau*

THE HURRICANE OF 1938

The week of September 19, 1938, had been unusually wet around Norwich, Connecticut. It had been raining steadily for days. Everyone knew that this time of year, with the changing of the seasons, often brought in storms and unsettled weather, so it didn't seem remarkable. By Tuesday, September 20, the ground was completely saturated and the Yantic, Shetucket, and Quinebaug Rivers, which feed into Norwich harbor, were swollen and had reached flood stage. As night came on, people kept a watchful eye on the rivers. Wednesday morning was cloudy again. There were reports of a hurricane down in Florida, but no one paid much attention. Hurricanes were something that happened down south and then veered off into the Atlantic when they got up to the Carolinas. Hurricanes simply were not something that happened in New England.

On the morning of Wednesday, September 21, 1938, everyone went about their business as usual, expecting just another rainy fall day. Gradually, as the day went on, the weather began to get worse—the clouds began racing across the sky. Then, without any of the warnings that modern weather forecasting provides today, a tremendous storm barreled through the area. Wind speeds reached 120 miles per hour in Norwich and New London. In Massachusetts, at the Blue Hill Observatory, a gust of wind was recorded at 183 miles per hour. The hurricane ripped through southeastern

Connecticut, calmed briefly during the eye of the storm, and then whacked the area once again. Then just as the winds finally died down, a powerful tidal surge washed away beach-side communities from Long Island to Nantucket. Water raced up the Thames River and washed right up into the city of Norwich, flooding the whole downtown area. Down by the Palace Theater the water rose almost to the marquee—over eleven feet high. According to newspaper accounts after the storm, Norwich was among the hardest hit places in Eastern Connecticut.

After the storm passed, the Rose City was devastated. The streets were blocked by fallen trees—the stately elm and chestnut trees—which had lined the streets of the city. Churches, mills, schools, and homes were battered and ripped apart. Dams were broken and bridges washed away. The people of Norwich were left to clean up and try to rebuild their lives.

Seventy-five years later, the '38 Hurricane remains the most powerful, destructive, and deadliest storm in New England history. What follows is a personal look at the hurricane as told through the stories of eyewitnesses who lived through the great storm. In the pages of this book people share their own memories of what they experienced that day and the impact the storm had on themselves, on their families, and on their communities.

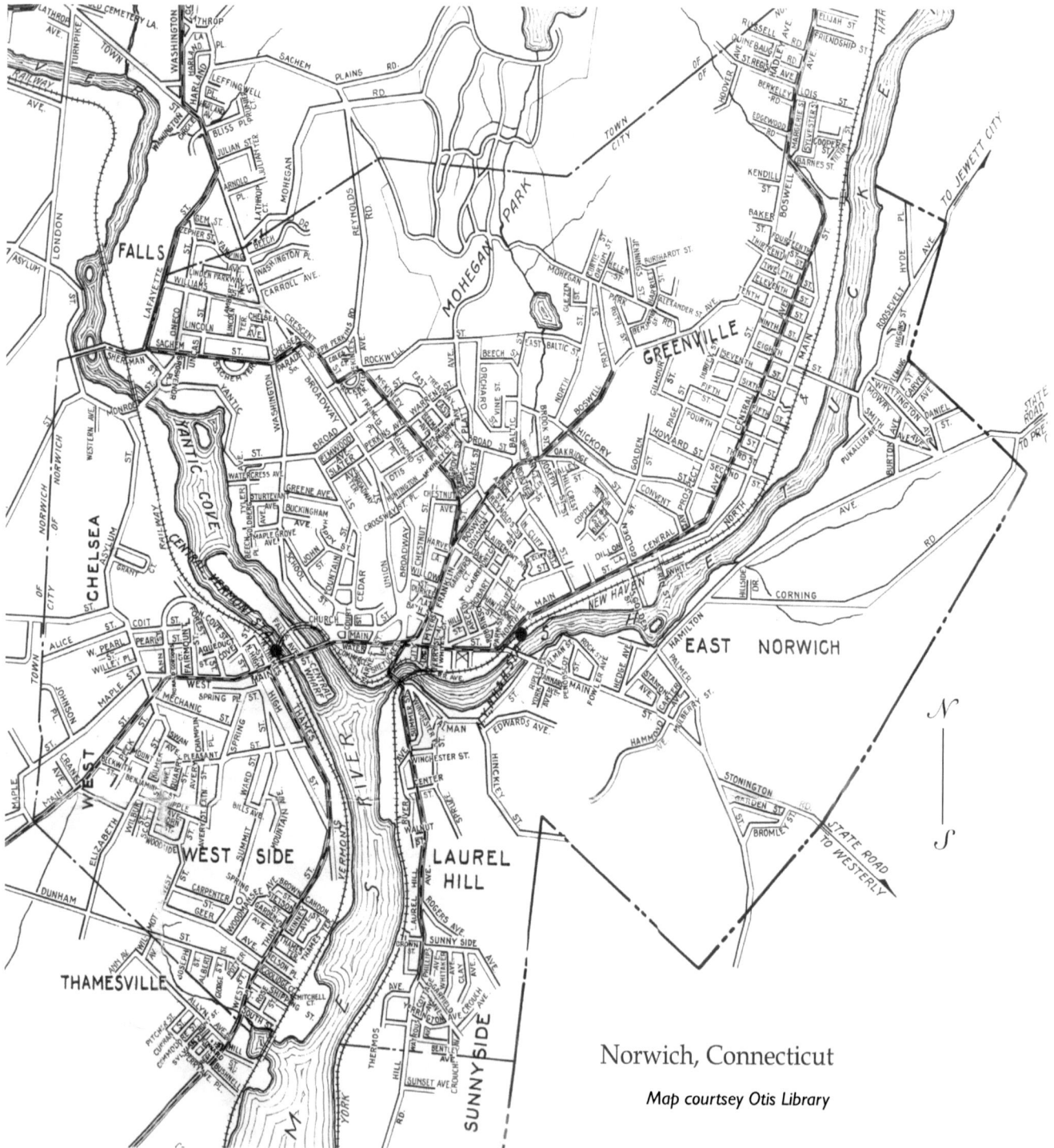

Norwich, Connecticut

Map courtsey Otis Library

NORWICH, CONNECTICUT

Irene (Duhaime) Radzvilowicz — born 1928
(see page 123)

My family lived at 157 Boswell Avenue in Norwich. I remember that morning was windy and rainy as I walked to the Boswell Avenue School. The weather got so bad that school was let out early before the storm really hit. My mother, Marie, came with my three brothers to meet me at school. She was very worried about us.

My father, Albert, had an auto repair shop over on Water Street. My mother decided we should all go downtown to meet up with him, so we could all be together during the storm. Well, it turned out that we didn't get far… My two older brothers, Albert and Raymond, headed out first. They only got as far as the park at the bottom of Boswell Avenue. The authorities were already stopping people from going down any further, because water was filling up the city. From there all the way to downtown, the city was flooded.

Then my mother, my brother Henry and I started out from our house. We walked up the street past my school at 139 Boswell Avenue, but we could only get as far as the intersection of Boswell Avenue, Broad Street, and Roath Streets. There were trees down everywhere blocking the way. I remember hearing the limbs cracking over our heads. This was near the old City Barn where they kept the sand trucks. We used to play in the big piles of sand they stored there. They still had a few horses in the barn, and I remember hearing them snorting and clunking their feet inside. There was a small shoe repair shop near there that was operated by an Italian man named Tony. When he saw us go by, he called us into his little shop to be safe. Once we were inside, we saw there were other people who had come in from the street, too. We all piled inside and moved to the back to get away from the big plate glass windows in the front. We soon realized there was no back door to his shop. There was no other way to get out should something happen to the front windows. Then we we all heard a big *roar*—a crunching sound that was louder than the wind. It was the sound of the roof of the Boswell Avenue School being blown off! We all stayed in his shop until the weather settled down. It was scary being there, but it was better than being out in the storm.

Meanwhile my older brothers tried another way to get further down into the city, but they were stopped again by firemen on Franklin Street, because of all the water coming up into the city. The water was flooding into the Palace Theater down by the railroad tracks and even into the Strand Theater (which we all called "The Scratch House") on Water Street. They never did get to my father's shop, which was across from the Auditorium Hotel, on the corner of Water and Market Streets. The firemen had set up a roadblock, and my brothers, being curious teenagers, just hung around the roadblock to find out what was going on.

Later in the day, my family all gathered together at our home and compared stories. My mother, my brother, and I got home first. A little while later, my two older brothers dragged in. Finally, my father made it home, too. It was then that we found out that my father had not even been in his workshop during the storm. He used to keep a fishing boat moored down in Ledyard, and someone who lived near there

> **We all heard a big roar—a crunching sound that was bigger than the wind.**

called my father and told him the water was getting really rough. They said he should come and pull his boat out. So he had taken off from his garage and headed up Laurel Hill to Ledyard. He didn't get any farther than the State Hospital. There used to be all these big trees along that road. My father said they were all falling left and right. A customer of my father's lived across from the hospital. They owned quite a bit of land right on the corner where you turn off to go to Preston. My father pulled into their yard, and they told him he could put his car in their garage. Somehow he got a funny feeling, and decided to pull his car out of their garage. He parked in their field, which was a good thing, because not long after that their garage went down. When the storm quieted down, my father left his car in their field and walked home. He couldn't drive, because all the big pine trees had come down like matchsticks in the road.

So we realized that we had all spent the day trying to go downtown to see my father. Yet all the while my father wasn't even at his workshop! We didn't know he wasn't there. If any of us had gotten to his shop, we would've been there all by ourselves with the water filling up the city. I guess we all had our own little adventures that day.

Several days later as things started to settle down after the storm, my father found his boat in Norwich. It had been washed down the river by the tidal wave. After the water receded, he found it down by the Shetucket Coal Company across from the Thermos. It was siting there up on the railroad tracks.

My father's workshop was on the ground floor of the Frisbee building near where all the wholesale dealers were. His shop made it through the storm okay since he was up a little higher from the flood.

Later, my brothers had to get shots since they had been down where the flood waters were in the city. Anyone who was down in that area had to get shots because of all the bacteria that got into the water from septic systems that had backed up.

Franklin Square, Norwich, Conn. — *Photograph by Edward & Mary Carlson*

John Fells — born 1922

I was sixteen years old and was at Norwich Free Academy (NFA) that day. Classes had ended at 1:30, and we had band rehearsal after school. In the middle of rehearsal, the lights went out in the rehearsal hall, so everyone took off for home. The weather had been wet and rainy off and on for the past couple of days. When we started for home, it began to rain again. Al Fitzgerald, Henry Lane, and I always walked home together. We walked down Crescent Street to Rockwell Street Extension. When we passed the D.A.R. Museum, we decided to take refuge on their big porch to wait out the shower. Al peddled papers in the morning, and he told us that he had read about the hurricane activity down south. Normally hurricanes moved up from Florida to Cape Hatteras, North Carolina, and then veered out to sea. No hurricane ever came north of Cape Hatteras. However, I guess this one missed a turn and came barreling up to New England.

The storm didn't seem to be letting up, so after waiting it out for a while, we decided to move along. As we started down McKinley Avenue, a car passed us and just after it went by, a tree fell across the road in front of it. Then we looked back and saw a tree laying on the D.A.R. porch, right where we had just been standing. We began to get a little worried. Henry said he was going to run and take a shortcut through the City Cemetery on Oak Street that led up to the top of the street where he lived. Al and I finally reached Al's house on the corner of McKinley and Grove. He ran into his house, and I continued up Grove Street to get to 254 Broad Street, where I lived. When I got to the top of Grove, I saw a huge tree laying across Broad Street blocking my path, so I decided to take a detour up Platte Avenue and circle around the other way. When I started up Platt, I ran into a blockade of cars with trees lying on them. I didn't realize the damage that the trees were causing even though I kept hearing trees falling right behind me. I seemed to be timing it just right; the trees kept just missing me. It was very weird.

Not being able to use the detour, I came back down to Broad Street and crawled under the big tree laying across the road. Just before my house, I had to cross the driveway that went down the side of the Turner Stanton Mill. I tried to cross it, but the wind caught me. It was so strong that it grabbed me, and held me. I was running in place, but not getting anywhere—like a cartoon character. I finally managed to run across the street and up the stairs to our house. I opened the door and ran inside. As soon as I closed the door, our chimney came crashing down over the doorway and onto the steps that I had *just crossed* to get into our house. My timing was right again! I looked out the window at the mill across the street and saw the corner of the roof flapping in the wind. Then, the whole roof just slid off the building and down into the mill yard.

Around 6:30 that evening, the storm moved on and the sun came out. It was a beautiful evening. Martial law was declared for Norwich. The National Guard was patrolling the downtown area by riding around in boats in Franklin Square, because the water had come up from the river and flooded the downtown area. The wind had even blown boats out of the water and way up onto the shore.

> The wind was so strong that it grabbed me, and held me— I was running in place like a cartoon character, but not getting anywhere.

The next morning Al Duhaime and I decided to go downtown to see what the city looked like. On the way, we stopped at Treat's Drug Store on Franklin Street. Our friend's family owned that store and another drugstore, Leone's, on the top of Main Street. Our friend asked us if we would do him a favor and go to their other drugstore, pick up some medicine, and deliver it to a lady on McKinley Avenue. We said, "OK" and headed up Bath Street. We only got as far as the courthouse when the National Guard stopped us. They asked where we were going. We explained what we were doing, and they told us that we needed to get a pass at the courthouse if we wanted to continue on. So we started out towards the courthouse, but then we looked around and noticed that Church Street was open. No one was around, so we headed up that way instead. We were eventually able to get the medicine and deliver it to the lady.

Then we continued on to NFA to see what was happening at the school. It was a mess. Trees were down all over the place. The football team was there helping with the cleanup using two-person saws and axes to cut up the trees.

My family was without electricity for about three weeks. That wasn't bad compared to many people. We were lucky. They had to get electricity back to the mill across the street from us, and we happened to be on the same line. Some people in Norwich were out for much longer than that. I know the last ones to get it were the folks up around Norwichtown. I heard they finally got power back just before Thanksgiving.

Mary (Perras) Grindstaff — born 1922

My family was living in a second-floor apartment on Franklin Street in the brick buildings near the Bulletin. I was fifteen years old and when I came home from NFA that day my mother,

There was cotton from the mill strewn all over the place, all the way from Yantic Street to the Poor Farm on the West Side.

Mini, sent me out to get my younger brother, Eli, who was at the Broadway School. I remember the wind was so strong that my umbrella blew inside out.

When Eli and I got home, the wind and rain were getting worse. There were bricks flying off the top floor of a building on Chestnut Street. My sister, Doris, had a dress out on the line, and she wanted to go out and get it. The storm was so bad that we told her to just leave it—even if it blew away. It wasn't worth trying to go get it. We could see the clock in the tower on City Hall from our house, and at one point we saw all four sides of the clock get blown out. The water from the Shetucket came up right to the door of our building.

The next day, Eli and I went out—without my mother knowing—to look around. The windows of the Bulletin were blown out and there were many windows blown out all along Franklin Street. It was just a mess: broken glass, branches, and bricks everywhere. We walked all around the city. Franklin Square was full of water. There were trees and wires on all the streets. We found a bunch of postcards floating in the water from a newspaper store up by the corner of Bath and Franklin. We collected some and brought them home. We went up to see the Falls Mill. My father, Venance Perras, worked there in the pick room, which was in the smaller stone building. Fortunately, he had been home during the storm, because the whole top floor of the main mill building blew off—bricks and all. There was cotton from the mill strewn all over the

The Falls Mill with spools of cotton thread exposed after the roof blew off.
— *photogrpah from "Hurricane Views," Bulletin-Record Printing Dept, 1938*

place—all the way from Yantic Street to the Poor Farm on the West Side. My brother and I decided we had better head home. We really got it from my mother when she found out we had been out wandering around the city.

I remember we had to get inoculated because of the flood water. I think we went to City Hall to get the shots. The whole city was chaotic. One thing was funny though. That storm did so much damage everywhere, yet after the storm had passed, my sister Doris' dress was still there hanging on the clothesline right where she had left it.

Joan (Montgomery) Keith — born 1938

My father, Ted Montgomery, owned Eldridge Hardware at 85 Water Street in Norwich. He told me that his store had been flooded so bad that after the storm he had to open his shop up on the roof of the building for three days while they cleaned out the store below.

Janet (Sanders) Burgess — born 1925

That morning my mother had told me it was going to be a bad day, so she would come and pick me and a friend up after school at the Broadway School, where I was in eighth grade. After school we waited and waited, but my mother never showed up. She couldn't get through. Eventually, some firemen came and escorted us to the firehouse down on Chestnut Street to wait out the storm. I remember the wind was so strong that it was hard to walk against it. Right next door to the firehouse was the old Broadway Theater. It was a large old building that extended from Broadway, where the main entrance was, all the way down the hill along Willow Street to Chestnut Street, where we were. We stood there with the firemen, watching the back

wall of the theater swaying back and forth above us. The firemen were trying to figure out if they should evacuate the firehouse in case the theater fell down on us.

The two bridges on West Main Street were flooded out during the storm. Some people were trying to set up a rope to pull a boat across, so they could get people over the flooded bridges. My two older brothers, Bill and Ken Sanders, swam across the river with the rope, but just as they got the rope across, the water got so bad and so strong that the rope and the boat were washed out. My brothers were lucky that they didn't get washed away, too.

I remember going down city after the storm. The Metropolitan Store, just below the Wauregan Hotel, had lost everything. Everything was flooded, and it smelled horrible. For a while, the whole city smelled of disinfectant. It smelled just awful!

Peter J. Pappas — born 1927

At the Hobart Avenue School where I was in the fifth grade, school usually let out at 3 o'clock. I remember the winds started really blowing, but the principal was waiting for word from the superintendent to let us out early. I was on the second floor of the school and had a good view out the window. There were lots of elm trees around our school, and the wind started picking them up and blowing them through the air. At 2:55, the

Top: Broadway Theater — *Ruth Tefft*
Bottom: Janet (Sanders) Burgess the day after the hurricane. — *Janet Burgess*

Broadway Theater Norwich, Conn.

teacher finally said we could go home. We were all thinking, if the wind is picking up those big elm trees, what was it going to do to us? There is a stone wall that separates the school yard from the Oak Street Cemetery. My older brother, Andrew, and I decided to follow the wall of the cemetery to cut over to where we lived on Acadia Street. The wind was blowing hard, so we crawled along the edge of the wall, hanging on to the stones to keep from blowing away. Suddenly, a strong gust of wind came up and blew over a big tree in the cemetery. The tree came up and wrapped in the roots was an old wooden casket box and a *skeleton* fell out of it! My brother and I had never seen a skeleton before. We thought it was the end of the world! I'll tell you, we ran like crazy to get home after that.

The tree came up and wrapped in the roots was an old wooden casket box and a skeleton fell out of it!

When we got home, my father, James, told us to go to bed, but we couldn't. We were too scared. Our house was made out of wood and it was shaking in the wind. Across the street was a brick house, and we had already seen the roof come off of that. If the roof was coming off a brick house, what was going to happen to ours? My family ended up going up the street to the Gaganis' house, which was sturdier than ours, and we waited the storm out with them.

Eleanor (Griffin) Miller — born 1926

I was about twelve years old and in the eighth grade at St. Patrick School. I was living with my aunt, Margaret Deschenes, on Court Street. My cousin and I always walked to school, and we would walk home for lunch. The day of the storm we walked home for lunch. On the way

Yantic cemetery
— *photograph by Ada K. Chase from the collection of Diane A. Norman*

11

The Broadway School

back to school we went through the center of Norwich, and we saw the water was coming up from the river. It was flooding the Palace Theater. We headed back up the hill to St. Patricks, and I remember that soon after we got back in class the storm started picking up and the wind began to howl. The nun had us all say a prayer together, and then she sent us home. Nobody had any idea the storm would be so bad. There was no warning. My cousin and I started to walk back to Court Street, but we never made it—there were trees down everywhere. Someone saw us and told us to come into their house to take shelter. We stayed there until later that afternoon when the storm finally subsided. Thinking about it now, it must have been horrible for my aunt. She was blind and had no idea where we were or if we were safe.

Stanley Isrealite — born 1925

My family lived on Joseph Perkins Road right next to the Manual Training building at NFA. In the fall of 1938, I was in the seventh grade at the Broadway School. I remember getting out of school that day. I was with my friend, Justin Dressler, who lived two houses down the road from me, and we always walked to school together. When we got outside, I saw all these trees and branches down everywhere. The wind was really blowing and things were flying around.

> I pulled her back inside the building. Just then the front wall of the school fell down right in front of us.

I said to Justin, "I don't think we should walk home now, look what's going on out here. We should go back into the school." So we headed back inside. We were standing near the front door of the Broadway School when suddenly the front door of the school flew open. Miss May Shields, one of the teachers, was there, and when the door blew open, she blew out the door! I reached out and grabbed her hand and she grabbed mine. I pulled her back inside the building and just then the front wall of the school fell down right in front of us. Fortunately, the wall blew out away from the school. There were bricks all over the place and a whole lot of noise—boy I remember that! We all hurried down into the cellar of the school: Ms. Shields, me, Justin, along with many other students. We waited down there until some firemen finally came to get us, and they escorted us all to City Hall. The police department was downstairs in City Hall at that time and there were a number of people who took shelter from the storm there along with us. We didn't know that it was a hurricane. We just knew that it was windy as hell.

I was in City Hall looking out the window and suddenly I saw my father, William, racing up Broadway. He had been at work at his jewelry store, Modern Jewelry, down city when he heard that the Broadway School had caved in, and he knew that I was in the school. I raced out after him. When I caught up to him, he turned around and just stared at me with great big eyes. I asked him, "Where you going?!" He just stood there shaking his head, and then finally he said, "I'm looking for YOU!"

My father and I went back inside City Hall. When we thought the storm had subsided enough, we started our journey home up Broadway. I'll never forget that walk home. I knew those streets so well. I walked them all the time. Broadway had been lined with *beautiful* big trees along both sides. But walking home that day it was like going through a jungle. Every tree was down. We had to climb up and down through the trees to get home. It was hard, especially for my father, who was an older man. I had to help him get through the downed trees. To me it was an adventure, but to my father it was a disaster.

When we finally got home, we saw that the roof on our house was gone. We went upstairs and opened the door to our attic and we could look up at the sky! It wasn't just our roof—many roofs were down. They were all over the place! My friend Justin's roof blew off, too. The city was a mess.

Somehow we managed to keep living in the house after the storm. We patched it up and just kept living there. We had no utilities. They were all shot, but we managed. Years before my father had built my mother, Cora, a cold room down in our basement that she used to store food she had canned in the summer. That was all we ate after the storm—my mother's jarred food.

Fortunately, we found out that my father had windstorm insurance. When he had built our house he had gotten an insurance policy, and he didn't even realize that he had coverage for windstorms. After the storm, the insurance guy called him and said, "Bill, you know you have insurance for this." So they came and put on a new roof and did other repairs for us, and the cost of it was all covered. That was pretty unusual. I don't think a lot of people were covered for wind damage back then.

Carol (Brand) Connor — born 1921

I was at NFA with my friend, Elaine Dickerman (whom everyone called Windy), and her two sisters, Jo and Betty. The four of us were watching the football team practice after school. I remember the wind was starting to blow hard. It was so exciting. I had on a "Gone With the Wind" dress, which I had purchased for $3.98 down at Porteous Mitchell. It had a 360 degree circle skirt. The wind was blowing my skirt, and my hair was flying around wild.

Carol, Jo, and Windy sitting on a downed tree in Carol's neighbor's yard.
— *Carol Connor*

After the practice, we walked home on Broadway. As we passed Dr. Driscoll's house—the big, white house with columns—the wind picked up even more. Along the sidewalk Dr. Driscoll had a wall with a wrought iron fence on top of it. I remember we had to hang on to that fence as we walked up the street because the wind was so strong.

Betty had left with her boyfriend, Pat, who was older and had a car. He said they were going to go down to go see the high water under the Laurel Hill Bridge. The three of us decided to go to see what was going on, too. We only got as far as the old Otis Library. There was a policeman there who stopped us and said, "You gotta get in, the storm is coming. You have to get in a shelter." We told him we would start heading back home, but the policeman told us we didn't have time for that. He told us to take shelter there at the library.

The telephone company was down near the Dime Savings Bank, so I decided to call home. When my mother answered the phone, I knew that I was in trouble. She said, "CAROL ELLEN BRAND, you get home right now!" Then I think our call was cut off. I went back to the library. There were many other people there. I saw some women kneeling and saying the rosary. It made me think how fast, in times of need, people remember to pray.

There was a Chinese laundry at the foot of Bath Street, where the parking lot for the Bulletin is now. I watched the couple who owned the laundry as they were leaving their store. The woman had her skirt tucked up high. The water was way up above her knees. She was carrying everything they valued in a basket on top of her head. The man, I think he was her husband, was following behind her. By that time the hurricane was really blowing full force, and the water was starting to creep up Bath Street.

I saw the roof of a tower—I believe it was from the Central Baptist Church—flying overhead, and the clock in the tower of City Hall blew out. The United Congregational Church lost one tower, and they never rebuilt it. All kinds of things were flying through the air—big things!

Once it quieted down a little, Windy, Jo, and I started to walk home. We had to climb over all the trees and branches in the road. The Dickermans lived over on Plain Hill, and Windy and Jo couldn't get back to their home. They ended up staying at our house on Rockwell Street for about three days. All of the trees around our house were blown down except for one cherry tree. Many of our neighbor's trees were down as well.

Don Gadle — born 1930

I remember the National Guard was trying to come up the street we lived on, Harland Road. They couldn't get through because of all the fallen trees. To get around the trees they were driving their trucks up on people's yards. My mother went out and was screaming at them because they were driving on top of our septic system with their *two and a half ton* trucks! Meanwhile my father, Joseph Gadle, was working in the Specialty Department at the Thermos on Laurel Hill. He couldn't get home after the hurricane and ended up staying there at the Thermos for the next three days.

The West Side

Albert Gualtieri — born 1923

I had just started my first year in high school that fall. I was on the cross-country team, and we were out in Mohegan Park when it started to get windy and cloudy. We went back to the school and took showers. By about 4 o'clock me and my friend, Billy Mandeville, started walking home. As we were walking down Washington Street towards the river, the trees started to fall around

People gathered around City Hall the day after the storm. Note the blown out clock tower.
— *photograph by Edward & Mary Carlson*

us. When we got to Falls Avenue, it was getting so bad that we decided to take shelter in the A&P store that was there at 73 West Main Street. There were about twenty people in the store waiting out the storm along with us. It just so happened that our cross-country coach, Matthew Sheridan, came in the store while we were there. Coach Sheridan was going out with Dolly Ferry, whose father, Frank Ferry, had an Italian store at 118 West Main Street near West Thames Street, over by Hertz Bros. meat market and Levi's Restaurant. Dolly worked at the store and Coach Sheridan was driving over to check on her. On his way, his car got stuck, so he came in the store with us. We all stayed in the A&P until about 6 o'clock that evening when the storm started to let up. I walked up West Main Street towards my home on Elizabeth Street. Then about an hour later, the sun came out and I decided to walk back into the city to see what was going on. When I got to the top of the hill, I saw there was about eight feet of water around the A&P store, right where we had been a few hours earlier.

Warren Burgess — born 1921

I was a senior in high school, and on the day of the hurricane I walked home after school. NFA was a good two miles from my house on Newton Street on the West Side of Norwich. I don't think we even knew that it was a storm. We thought it was just a rainy day, but by the time I got home, it was pretty bad. We lived up on high ground. I remember looking out the window and

Trees down on Washington Street. —photograph by Ada R. Chase from the collection of Diane A. Norman

17

US Finishing Company in Greeneville showing roof damage and flooding.
—*photograph by Ann MacDonald*

seeing the roof of the barn across the road come off. It almost landed on our front yard. I was able to convince my family to go down into the basement. We weathered it out down there. I had a dog, Rover, who was tied out by his doghouse. I remember I had to go out to retrieve him during the storm.

When we finally came out of the basement, we saw trees down and branches all over the place. We had no electricity for about two weeks. Our house was all electric, so we had no means of cooking or heating up food. Our next door neighbors had an old three-burner oil stove, so we got together with them so we could at least have one hot meal a day. The rest of the time we ate cold food or whatever we could get.

I'm not sure if NFA closed, but I stayed out of school for about two weeks. I had a chance to work in Greeneville at the US Finishing Company, which had been really devastated by the storm and the flood. One of our neighbors was a foreman for a construction company, and he offered me a chance to work on the cleanup and rebuilding at US Finishing for the next two weeks. There was no problem with missing school, I suppose because of the urgency of the situation.

My father, Foster Burgess, was self-employed. He had his own business as a radio repair man. He also had an appliance store in Norwich for a time, Burgess Sales and Service in Washington Square. Back then everyone had a radio with an antenna. All the antennas came down during the hurricane. I remember he was very busy putting them all back up in the weeks after the storm. He had so much work for a while that I was helping him out, too.

Lucy (Bullard) Cilley — born 1931

I was seven years old in 1938, and I attended the East Great Plains School. The weather was getting very windy and rainy, so Miss Peterson sent us home. No one really knew what was going on. I remember having trouble getting the door of the school open, because of the wind. I was with my friend, Janice, and we started up Pine Street. Janice's grandmother met us, and then my aunt, Alice Leffingwell, who lived right over the wall from the school, came and got me. By that

time, it was very windy and raining hard. We went to my aunt's house at 675 West Main Street. There used to be many big elm trees along West Main Street, and one of those big trees fell right on my aunt's house and took off one of the first floor bedrooms and half of her porch. We were in the dining room when it fell, so we were OK, but it made an awful lot of noise! There were people, who had been trying to drive by our house, but the street was blocked by trees. Those strangers started coming into my aunt's house and took shelter with us until late evening, when the wind subsided and everyone could walk home. My aunt had to have canvas put up to cover the part of her house that had been hit.

My mother, Ida, was working as a home nurse for Dr. Freeman, and whenever she was away my mother's two spinster sisters often helped take care of us. That day my mother was working for a patient on Old Salem Road. She wasn't far away, but she had to stay with her patient for a few days, so my sisters and I stayed with my aunt for about three days.

Meanwhile, my father, Rodger, had taken my older sister Mary to the Springfield Fair that day. We didn't see them for three days. They had to live in their car. There were so many trees down that they couldn't go anywhere. My father told us that there was a woman who lived near where they were stranded who had invited them to come into her house and she fed them.

The Thames River two hours before the storm.
— *photograph by Ada R. Chase from the collection of Diane A. Norman*

Washington
Street
—*photograph by
Ada R. Chase
from the
collection of
Diane A. Norman*

Top: Car damage in Norwich.
— *Janet Burgess*

Left: Norwich dock.
— *photograph by Edward & Mary Carlson*

Marie (Tedeschi) Crane — born 1930

I was in class at the High Street School the day of the storm. The school had those big tall windows and I remember the windows in our classroom started rattling. It was creepy hearing them rattle in the wind. At some point, a tree fell on the front of the school, but even then they still didn't dismiss us. We were sent home at the regular time, 3 o'clock. They let us out the side door, since that tree was down in front. No one warned us that this was a bad storm and that we should go straight home. They just let us go... I walked with a group of kids down High Street. I was the only one who had to turn off to go down to Thames Street. There was a set of stairs that led down from High to Thames. As I went down the stairway, I was literally hanging on to the rocks in the wall, because the wind was blowing so hard. Then there was a gas station that I had to walk by. I was petrified because there was nothing there to hang on to. I didn't know how I would get by that open space. Fortunately, my uncle happened to be driving my mother, Vincenca, home. He stopped, picked me up, and drove us to our house at 137 Thames Street. Our house was right along the Thames River. From up there, we could see all the boards from Dawley Lumber Yard floating down the river. The wind was blowing so hard we couldn't keep the door to our house closed. We had an old wooden icebox that my father, Santo, pushed up against the door to try to keep it closed, but, even with that, it blew in again. Finally, he took some boards and nailed them across the door to keep it shut.

I had two brothers, Herman, who was twelve, and Bruno, who was ten. Bruno delivered the evening newspaper, the *Norwich Record*. After school that day, he went down North Main and up Church Street to get over to the *Bulletin* to pick up his papers when a woman told him he shouldn't be out in the storm. He tried to head home, but couldn't get back across the bridges— the river had flooded over them! All of my aunts lived on Washington Street, so Bruno went there and stayed overnight with my Aunt Henrietta Tedeschi. My other brother, Herman, had stayed with someone over on Mt. Pleasant Street until the storm was over, but he made it home that night. We didn't have a phone, so there was no way for us to know where my brothers were. My mother was a very excitable woman, and she went bananas that day.

We rented the first floor of a three-story house from the Longos. During the storm, the wind blew the whole roof off our house. We didn't know it had happened, even though we were inside the house at the time! The wind was so noisy, and I guess since there was another floor above us, we didn't realize it had blown off until after the storm passed. I remember seeing our roof laying in the road. The whole roof was laying there—in one piece.

The following day, my father went out to see my aunt. He needed to get over the bridges on West Main Street, but both of the bridges were still under water. They were using a little rowboat to get people across, so he actually rode a boat across the bridge. The city was giving out tetanus shots, and my brothers were told they needed to get them. I remember some group was giving out food for a few days, and our family got some beef stew.

Even now, all these years later, whenever there is a windstorm, I get very, *very* nervous. I guess it's because of that hurricane in 1938. Now whenever we hear that a hurricane is coming, we prepare. We don't just casually fluff it off. We have seen ourselves how bad these storms can be and how much damage they can do.

Greeneville

Tom LaFreniere — born 1928

I was ten years old and in the seventh grade at the Greeneville School. That was the Central Avenue school, the original Greeneville School. Around 2 o'clock that afternoon, our class was doing round and square dancing on the top floor of the school with Miss Shugrue. All of a sudden, the winds came up and blew the roof right off of the school. That roof was made out of copper or tin and it was peeled off by the wind, just like a banana. The rain was pouring in and the teacher said, "I guess I have to let you children go home." So we all ran out in all directions—helter skelter—with no supervision.

I lived at Twelfth and South Main Street, about five or six blocks up from the school. There were trees all along Central Street, and they were all coming down. I was afraid I would get hit by a tree. I knew there were no trees in the alleys, so I decided to run through the back alleys to get home. I could see the dam and the water was coming up high over the road. My father, Wilfred LaFreniere, owned Bids Tavern at 578 North Main Street. The tavern sits close to the Shetucket River, and the cellar of that tavern was flooded with water.

Raymond R. Carlson Jr. — born 1918

The following was submitted by Ray's daughter, Rosalyn (Carlson) Lachapelle.

When the 1938 Hurricane struck, my father, Ray Carlson, was the only one in their home on St. Regis Avenue in Greeneville. He headed for the Greeneville School on Central Avenue to get his little sister, Joyce. It was quite a hike from the old brick Greeneville School to St. Regis Avenue. Once he got to the school, he saw several other little children who he knew that lived nearby. He decided to take them home, too. He tied a rope around his waist and then around the waist of each child, so they wouldn't blow away in the wind. Then, when he reached the home of one of the children, he would untie them, shove them in their door, and then move on to the next house. Once he had brought all the other children to their homes, he and Joyce eventually made it back to their home.

> He tied a rope around his waist and then around the waist of each child, so they wouldn't blow away in the wind.

Ray's father, Ray Carlson Sr., was driving bus for the Connecticut Bus Company. He drove as far as he could until the trees all started coming down and blocking the road. He couldn't drive any further, so Ray Sr. and all his passengers just abandoned the bus over on Sachem Street and set off on foot. Ray's brother, Harry, spent the storm trapped at NFA in the library.

John Buzenski — born 1924

I was thirteen years old, and I had just started my first year of high school at NFA just a few weeks before the storm. The wind was blowing like crazy, and my old grammar school, the Greeneville School, had its roof blown off. We were all excited and wondering, "What's going on?!" I lived on Sixth Street, and there used to be a Union Hall on the corner of Sixth and North Main. Across the street was an apartment house and downstairs from it was a candy store that sold soda and whatnot. Me and a lot of other kids from the neighborhood hung out there during the storm. While we were there, the roof from Union Hall, across the street from us, blew right off. The owner of the store told us all to stay away from the big windows in the front in case they broke, so we tried to stay towards the back of the store.

When the eye of the storm came over, the sun came out and everything was quiet. We thought the storm must be over, but, no, no…! Pretty soon it started blowing again.

I wasn't fearful, I was excited. After the hurricane, the man who owned the drugstore that was on the corner of Seventh and Central invited all of us kids in the neighborhood in for free ice cream. The power was out and his ice cream was melting, so rather than let it spoil, he invited us in and gave it to us for free! I tell you, that was quite a treat for me. My father had died when I was five years old, my mother was a widow, and we never had much.

Jack Buchanan, a friend of mine from grammar school, talked me into going down to the Eighth Street Bridge. We had heard the water was really high, so we went there and stood watching all

this debris coming down the river. We crossed over to the Preston side of the bridge and foolishly decided to go down to the steelwork under the bridge. We walked across it to the middle of the river and from there we watched all the stuff going by—trees, barrels, and all kinds of junk floating down the river. The water was only about two feet from the bottom of the steel structure where we were standing. Well, you know what happened to that bridge just the next day. The whole thing was carried away! I guess we were lucky. I never told my mother I did that! After the Eighth Street bridge washed out, they put up a temporary bridge—just a walking bridge—so people could walk from Greeneville to Preston. Eventually, they built the new bridge for cars.

After the hurricane, we had to get tetanus shots, which were given out for free by the city. Right after we got our shots, these old Polish men called over to us. They were out cutting trees, and they told us to come grab one end of their bucksaw to help them. They said the exercise would help our arms from getting sore after the tetanus shot. So that's what we did; we started cutting trees down with them. There had been a lot of elm trees along both sides of Central Avenue, and the wind had blown them all down into the road. It was a mess everywhere.

The remains of the Eighth Street Bridge.
— photograph by Ann MacDonald

We went down to the steelwork under the bridge and walked across it to the middle of the river.

John Armen (Armenakas) — born 1921

That afternoon I was working after school in the print shop at the Academy in the Bradlaw (MT) building. We were looking out the window and could see the wind blowing. There were three big elm trees in the back, and suddenly, one of those elms came down. Then we saw the second tree come down, and then the third one. We got all excited, and Mr. Bradlaw, the head of the department, sent us home.

The day after the storm, I went back to NFA and was part of the cleanup crew that helped cut up the trees that had fallen on the field. Those elm trees fell right on top of the bleachers. We were out there working with handsaws clearing the place out. For me, it was exciting. I was just thrilled to be a part of it. There was never a point when the thought of danger crossed my mind.

The Eighth Street Bridge washed out in that storm. That was a mad river then. They put up a temporary bridge across the canal at Eighth Street, a small wooden bridge with wooden handrails.

You know, we used to go swimming in that river. We would go down to Shetucket Lumber on Golden Street Extension where the river was fairly narrow. The East Side was just across the river. We would take off our clothes, hold them in our hands over our heads, and walk across the river at low tide. There was a gang on the East Side that was always in battle with the gang on our side. Our gang was called the "Jazbow Dukes," and we were very organized. We had the use of a two-car garage on the corner of Boswell and Hickory Streets. The family there owned a little grocery store, and they let us use their garage. We had a Ping-Pong table in there and a radio. In the store we kept a gallon of strawberry and chocolate syrup, and we had our own dishes. We would buy ice cream from the store and then use one of our syrups to make ourselves banana sundaes. Back then every section of town had a group. The girls' gang up the street from us was called the "Kit Kats."

Nicholas Topalis — born 1930

I remember being at recess that morning at the Greeneville School. I was pointing out to the other kids how the clouds were racing through the sky really fast. After recess when we went back in the school and were sitting there watching huge trees falling outside. The teachers released class early, and my big brother, Peter, came to get me. It was about three-quarters of a mile to our house from school. We had to walk up a big hill to get home, and we couldn't make it. We kept getting blown down, so we had to go around and find another route where the wind wasn't so strong. When we finally got home, we saw that several windows in our apartment were blown

Victim of the "Big Wind"

out. We were trying to stuff things in the windows to keep the wind and rain from coming inside. All the streets were completely impassible for a while. Many people burned wood back then, and I can tell you, after that storm, they had firewood galore!

Edward Zizulka — born 1929

I was in the fourth grade at the Smith Avenue School, and we were sent home early that day, about noon, I think. To us kids, it was just another wet and windy day. I lived on Roosevelt Avenue, so I didn't have far to go. I don't remember seeing anything really bad on my way home from school, other than a few small trees uprooted and some trash being blown about. Later sometime in the late afternoon, a large tree in our front yard was blown over and crashed into the house. After that, we went to my aunt's home up the street, and we rode out the storm there. When the power went out, my aunt and uncle used oil lamps and candles for light. It became quite scary, because their house really creaked and groaned with each gust of wind. Everyone was worried that the storm would tear off the roof or that the windows would break.

Due to the heavy rain preceding the storm, my father, Joseph, had gone to Occum, where my mother's parents, Joseph and Anna Chrzan, lived. He was going to help them prepare in case there was flooding. Their place did flood, and he was trapped there with them. They rode out the storm on the second floor of their house, along with their chickens, which they had brought

He was trapped there with them. They rode out the storm on the second floor of their house along with their chickens.

in before the water arrived. I don't remember just how long he was there, but he had a very difficult time returning home due to all the roads being blocked by fallen trees, downed power lines, and the flooding. When he did return, he brought us all the news about what had happened and what he had seen in the Norwich area.

The Eighth Street Bridge washed out, so they had to put up a wooden pedestrian bridge across the river. I remember being scared to walk across that bridge. It was very close to the water and it moved up and down as people walked over it. In spite of that, we used it since the only other option would have been to walk all the way to the East Side via Hamilton Avenue and use the Preston Bridge to get into the city.

From my view overlooking the Shetucket River, I remember seeing buildings and even some dead animals being swept along in the high floodwaters of the river in the days just before and after the Hurricane of 1938.

Scene from New Haven, Conn.
— *photograph from "A Photographic Record of the New England Hurricane and Flood, New England's Greatest Disaster," by The Connecticut Circle Magazine*

Josie (Wujcik) Piechowski — born 1935

My parents, Josephine and Frank Wujcik, lived in Greeneville on the corner of Erin and North Main Street. I was pretty small during that storm, but remember a big tree on the corner near our house blew down. My aunt's mother-in-law owned several apartments down on White Street, just down the hill from us. Those apartments were located right on the water, and wWhen the river came up, it flooded into the cellars of those buildings. Everyone who lived down there came up to stay at our house, since we were on higher ground.

My mother was *very* pregnant, and she went into labor during the storm with all of those people there in her house. My father headed downtown to find Dr. Suplicki so he could help my mother with the baby. He finally found him at Lerou's Drug Store, at 289 Main Street. Dr. Suplicki was sleeping there, because he couldn't get back to his home. Somehow my father and Dr. Suplicki made it back to our house, and my mother gave birth to my sister, Barbara, early the next day. Because she was born during the storm, we always called my sister the "Hurricane Kid."

Taftville

Roger Marien — born 1927

I lived in Taftville and attended the Sacred Heart School in the seventh grade. I remember we were in class that morning and it got dark—very, *very* dark. Then, it started to rain and the wind started to come up. The classroom I was in had big windows that faced south, which was the direction the storm was coming from. Those were great big windows and the wind was making them crackle. They were shaking and vibrating, so the nun, who was teaching my class, said we had to close the windows. To close the windows you needed a long pole with a gadget on the top to push them up. Before we could get the pole, the nun who was the principal of our school suddenly started running up and down the halls, knocking on the doors of the classes, and telling the teachers, "Dismiss the children immediately!"

> **Suddenly, the nun started running up and down the halls of the school. She was knocking on the doors of the classes and telling the teachers, "Dismiss the children immediately!"**

I lived close to the school at 49 South A Street. To get to my house, I had to walk across the outfield of a baseball field. As I walked through the field, sticks and even small stones were flying

The Edward Chappell Company on Central Wharf in Norwich.
—photograph by Ada R. Chase from the collection of Diane A. Norma

by. It was scary. Some of the kids, especially the younger ones, were falling down. I had to help a few of them get back up again.

When I managed to get home, my father, Joe, asked, "Where's your sister Terry?" I told him I didn't know. So he went out in the field to find her and brought her home. By that time, more and more branches and trees were falling. There were other children who were trying to walk to their houses along South A Street. Some of the kids couldn't go any further due to all the trees on the ground. My father went back out again and gathered up twenty children and brought them all into our house. The storm was so loud. It was scary for everyone. We could hear trees falling outside. Some of the children were crying. My father and my mother, Irene, were trying to calm them down. They gave them a snack and tried to keep them amused.

Eventually, the storm subsided, and the winds died down. My father made a decision to bring each of the children home himself. All of those children lived along South A Street. In those days everyone knew each other on the street, so he knew where each of the children lived. He was taking one child by one hand and one child in the other, and walking those two children to their doors. Then he would return to our house to get two more. In order to get the children home, they had to walk under and over fallen branches. In some places, if the street was blocked, they had to walk through backyards. He did that for all twenty kids. The last child he brought home was a girl by the name of Lorraine White. He brought her home and knocked on her door. Lorraine's mother was so relieved that my father had brought her daughter home safe that she invited him inside and told him she couldn't thank my father enough. She said, "Anything you see in my house, you can have as thanks for bringing my daughter home." My father said that wasn't necessary. He was just glad he was able to get her to her home.

We were without power for several days, but we always had water, because our water came from the water system for Ponemah Mill, which ran under the streets. My mother worked the second shift at Ponemah, and my father worked there as a mechanic. for the first shift, from 6 o'clock until 2 o'clock. The mill had sent him home early that day, because they had water damage on some of the lower floors. There was a bridge on the Norwich side of Ponemah that went into Lisbon. That bridge was knocked down, and the dam in Baltic got knocked out, too.

Arthur Bolieau — born 1931

I was eight years old in the fall of 1938, and I had made my First Holy Communion just that very morning.

Arthur on the morning of the storm.
— *Arthur Bolieau*

My aunt, my brother and sister, and I were all coming back home from Sacred Heart Church on Providence Street in Taftville when we got caught in the storm. I still had on my bow tie, short pants, and high socks. I was soaking wet in that little suit. The wind was blowing the windows in on the houses, and talk about the debris…! There was all kinds of stuff all over the place. It was pretty bad.

We lived on North Fifth Avenue. The wind took the roof right off of our house. We had quite a going on there with that, so we went and stayed with our neighbors. The rain was really heavy and everything got soaked. We lost a lot of our things. I remember seeing people walking up the street and the wind just blew them away. The signs from the front of all the stores were lying all over the street. Cars were all twisted up. The cars were being moved all over the place

by the wind—you could actually see the cars being pushed around! The thing that amazed me were the big trees—several feet across—that were just blown right over. Some stone walls were knocked down, too. People had all their garbage cans out that day, and they were blown all over the street. The cans were rolling around the road. Everybody's belongings were blown all over the place. Sacred Heart Church had a lot of damage. Ponemah Mill took a beating; they had a lot of busted windows and shingles blown off, and half the dam gave way. The Baltic dam and the Occum dam gave way, too.

Laurel Hill

Gerald Dufault — born 1931

I am eighty-two years old now, but back in 1938 I was just seven years old. We lived up on Rogers Avenue off of Laurel Hill. It was balmy that morning as we walked to the Laurel Hill School. By the time my cousin came to pick me up after school that day, the weather was starting to get rough. My family rented an apartment on the middle floor of the big white house that was owned by the Sukowskis. I saw a limb, about two foot in diameter, come down in our

The remains of the Freight House.
— *photograph by Ada R. Chase from the collection of Diane A. Norman*

yard, and there were lots of trees down all over the street. From our apartment, I could see right across to the Thames River. I could see the tides coming in, and I watched as the water came up over the railroad tracks and all around the Dawley oil tanks. It came up to Dawley Lumber and washed a bunch of their lumber away. I remember seeing it all floating down the river. Out on the streets there was green copper wire everywhere.

That house we lived in is built right on a cliff. We were afraid the whole house would blow away. If you lived in that house during a hurricane like that, you'd be afraid it would blow away, too! During the center of the storm when it quieted down, we went next door to my aunt's house and waited out the rest of the storm.

East Side

Manuel (Manny) Cardoza Jr. — born 1929

We lived on the East Side of Norwich at 93 Talman Street. I remember it had rained and rained and rained for about three days before the hurricane hit. We were in class at the Bishop School on East Main Street late that morning, and we were watching the water start to rise

on to Duwell Field, which was a playground and baseball field adjacent to the Bishop School. By early afternoon, we kept watching it rise and then the wind started picking up. Miss Shugrue, my fourth grade teacher, said, "We're going to have to let you out early." We all thought, "That's cool!"

All these trees were falling, so me and my friends, Billy Rizzuto and Freddy Plant, thought it would be a good idea to cut up through Duwell field, up to the woods, and watch the trees fall. We cut back through the woods and came back towards the Preston City Bridge. We were up in the woods watching the trees fall. It was crazy! We were sitting there saying, "Look at that big one over there. That one's going to fall!" We were having ourselves a good time. We didn't know any better. Finally, we came down out of the woods and headed home.

When we got home, my mother, Senherenia (everyone called her Shuma) jumped on us. Apparently, my mother and Mrs. Rizzuto had gone to the school to get us, but just as they were coming down one way to find us, me and my friends were going the other way, up to the woods. We tried to tell them that we took a shortcut home, but I had a good talking to from my mother about that.

The wind was crazy—blowing and hollering. Whenever we had storms, my mother always said that we had to be quiet; we'd just sit there and be quiet in the dark—no lights, no nothing.

She would go by the window and pray with her rosary. So we just sat there in the dark. It was about 12 o'clock. There was nothing to do, so I ended up falling asleep. When I woke up, it was about 4 o'clock and I remember it was calm outside. I looked outside, and there were branches all over the place. From my house, we could see the trestle behind the Palace Theater. That trestle was pretty high. We used to dive off it in the summertime. Well, that afternoon we were looking at it and the water was about seven to eight feet up from the bottom of the trestle and there were trees and everything coming up against it. We were sitting there watching it, waiting for the trestle to go. We just sat there for about an hour watching everything pile up against it. I remember seeing a small shed coming down the river and it had four live chickens on top of it. There were all kinds of trees coming down and piling up against that trestle. We watched it until it got dark. When we went to bed, we thought, "Aw, that trestle is going to go down in the middle of the night while we're sleeping. We're going to miss it!" The first thing we did in the morning was to check if the was bridge still there. We kept looking at it over the next few days. We thought, "That bridge has got to go. It's just gotta go!" It took about two or three days for the water to finally go down, and that trestle stayed right where it was. They must have built that good.

Flood waters around the railroad trestle bridge. —*photograph by Edward & Mary Carlson*

The second day after the storm, my mother told me to go down to the Ferry Brothers grocery store on Main Street across from the Flatiron building. My mother had traded with them for ages. She had a charge account there, and she would pay one or two dollars a week on it. I remember there were soldiers in town then. They were stopping us from going downtown. So I went down back by the tracks to the place they called Little Italy, down by Bath and Water Streets. That was by Angelo's on Water Street where they sold tomato pies—pizza pies. There were a lot of businesses down there, the Strand Theater and Eldridge Hardware. I snuck down that way and

Debris washed on the tracks of the railroad bridge.
— *The Bulletin*

then cut back up to get to Ferry Brothers. The stores downtown like Beit Brothers and the Mohican Market had been flooded, but Ferry Brothers was up higher, so they had stayed dry. The store was completely crowded with people. I went in and asked if they had any meat. The man went in the back, grabbed some meat, and wrapped it up for me to bring home for my mother.

Then a short way up the street I saw everyone standing in line at the church on Main Street. I'm not sure which church that was. It isn't there anymore. I decided to stand in line along with everyone else. They were handing out baked bean sandwiches. I will never forget that. That was the first time I ever had a baked bean sandwich! That was back when the big furniture store, Silberman's, was there. There were a lot of good stores around there, like Porteous Mitchell and Tongren's shoe store and clothing stores like H. A. Bruckners, Feister-Raucher, and Trachtenberg's.

School was out about a good week or so. That was OK with us. We were having a good time, playing up in the woods and wandering around to look at the city. The Auditorium Hotel was at the bottom of Water Street right next door to the Strand Theater. I remember that out in front of the Auditorium Hotel there was a huge boat—a twenty-five footer, sitting there in the street. Right in the middle of Franklin Square there was another boat—right in the middle of the square. Franklin Square had about seven to eight feet of water during the storm. There was a culvert that went way up under Franklin Square. I guess the water just rose up from there. There was a lot of water everywhere. For about a week the river was just tremendous. There were branches and trees and everything floating down with it. Our school was OK, but some of the kids from the Broadway School had to come over to our school since theirs had been damaged.

Boat in
front of the
Auditorium
Hotel.
— *photograph
by Ada R.
Chase from
the collection
of Diane A.
Norman*

My two older half-brothers, James and Philip Marceline, were in the CCC camp in Voluntown, Camp Lonergan. They came to Norwich to help with the cleanup after the storm. My friends and I were just kids and didn't pay much attention. We were just playing and having a good time. It was quite an experience.

Ann (Roessler) MacDonald — born 1922

I had been babysitting for a lady on North Cliff Street in Norwich. The woman had gone down to the Mohican Store to buy some groceries, but then came back very quickly. She said that Franklin Square was full of water, and she hadn't been able to get anywhere downtown. She told me I should try to go home. I tried to call my parents to let them know I was on my way, but when I tried to use the telephone across the street, they weren't letting any calls through. It was very staticky and there wasn't even an operator answering.

I went to the Preston Bridge to cross the river. When I got there, a National Guardsman stopped me. He said he wasn't supposed to let anyone cross. I pleaded with him, "I have to go home! You have to let me cross." I finally got him to agree. He said, "OK, I'll let you go now, but run as fast as you can." So I ran and got across. Then I went up East Main Street to Hamilton Avenue, climbing over trees the whole way.

My father, Charles, was a bus driver for the Trolley Car Bus Company. His bus got trapped by trees on one of the side streets in Greeneville. He locked up his bus where it was, took his things and his change carrier, and then walked all the way down to the Preston Bridge. They let him cross, too. It was dark by the time it he got back home.

At our house on Daniel Street, the rain was so heavy it kept coming in under the doors. I remember my mother, Georgianna, had to keep mopping it up over and over again.

Art Prodell had a little grocery store over on Hamilton Avenue where he had an ice cream cooler and cabinets with candy and such. After the storm, we went down there to see if maybe he still had a loaf of bread left that we could buy. We bought canned goods, bread, and, of course, cigarettes. I guess everyone was doing the same thing. Art's supply only lasted so long until he was sold out.

Down in Franklin Square when all the water had finally drained out, they had to put lime everywhere as a disinfectant. They sprinkled it on everything. All of the store owners were trying to clean up and were sorting through their supplies. They were putting everything that had been damaged in the flood outside on the sidewalks into big barrels that were to be dumped, but then of course there were some people who were going through those barrels to try to retrieve anything they could for themselves.

Faith Jennings — born 1918

That afternoon I took my friend, Catherine Meyers, who lived near me, and we drove up to Occum. By the time we got over the Preston Bridge, all the trees were thrashing around. Catherine's husband wasn't home yet. She was nervous and didn't want to stay in her house alone, so she came up here to stay with me. My mother, Eva, was here with the twins, Richmond and Annie. We all stayed inside watching the trees come down. We had several big maples around here, and I'd guess at least three or four of them came down.

My brother George owned Jennings Studio, over near the Post Office. When he heard about the storm, he drove down to Mumford's Cove by Bluff Point. He had a boat down there, and he wanted to secure it. When he was coming back, the wind was wild. He made it only as far as Poquetanuck. He couldn't drive any further. The trees were down in the road front and back, blocking his path, so he had to walk or get rides when he could. My brother finally made it back to his house. He was glad to get there. He had been really worried about his wife and their baby, who was just three months old at the time.

Flooding in
Franklin Square.
— *photograph by
Edward & Mary
Carlson*

That afternoon when the storm subsided a little bit, we walked down Roosevelt Avenue and over to East Main Street. There were trees down everywhere. Everybody seemed to be walking around to see what had happened. We made it down to the Mohican Store. Franklin Square was flooded. I was taking pictures all the time. I remember I took one shot where I put the camera on the sidewalk. It must have been about 6 o'clock or so, because it was getting pretty dusky. I might have given it a time exposure—and I got a picture showing the flood in Franklin Square. I didn't think it was a great print, but the Bulletin was wild for it and they published it. That was as far as we could go, so we turned around and headed home.

We were lucky at our house; other than the trees, we only lost one pane of glass in our back porch area. We made out pretty good. We didn't have electricity for about three weeks, but we had kerosene lamps on hand and my mother had a big, black, oil-burner stove in the kitchen. That was a tremendous storm. Even now I can picture that day. My mother was sitting right

here where I am sitting now. She was all nervous. I was running around upstairs looking out the windows as the trees were crashing around us…

Blanche (Cimikoski) Armen — born 1928

I was ten and at school on Smith Avenue when the wind started to get worse. That afternoon, the teacher told us class was dismissed and everyone had better hurry up and get home. I lived at 43 Roosevelt Avenue, and my two friends, Sasha and Ruthie, lived close to me. The three of us walked home together, hugging each other to keep from being blown away. We saw our neighbor Mr. Combies driving by in his car. He stopped and said he would drive us in his car as close to our homes as he could get. He dropped us at our neighbors, and from there we cut through the backyards. Just as I got into my house, our famous pear tree fell down. That tree always had big, beautiful Bartlett pears. Being late Spetember, the tree was heavy with fruit and it just fell over. That tree was the pride and joy of my grandfather, Walenty Cimikoski. He was so upset that his tree was gone. He knew all the Polish swear words, and he sure used them that day!

View down to
Franklin Square
from Franklin
Street.
— *photograph by
Edward & Mary
Carlson*

My mother, Blanche, was at work in her beauty shop, Lorraine's, in Franklin Square right above the United Fruit Store. I called her, and we talked about the Eighth Street Bridge, which was right down the hill from our house. She had heard reports that the waters were coming up to the bridge and officials were saying that people shouldn't use it. My mother wasn't sure how she was going to get home, but she said she would be fine. Meanwhile, I stayed at home, as more and more rain poured down and more trees started to fall.

When the water started to come up to Franklin Square, my mother decided to leave her shop. It was getting dark as she was going up Cliff Street. She thought if she could just get up the hill, then she would be safe, but the wind was too strong. It picked her up and slammed her down onto the ground, breaking her shoulder. Someone in a house nearby knew her and saw her get pushed down by the wind. They brought her into their house and took care of her. One of our neighbors was there with his pickup truck, and once my mother was cleaned up a little bit, he drove her home. My father, Henry, didn't come home for a few days. He was at work at the State Hospital. He had to stay there a couple of nights, because the power at the hospital was off.

The next day my mother told us to walk up to the little store on Hamilton Avenue to see what we could find to keep us going for a few days. We went and bought out the grocery store. We had to, since there were six of us in the house. The power was off for while, but fortunately we could use my grandfather's old-fashioned black wood stove in the kitchen. We had a well that we could drop a bucket down, and I think we still had a water pump in the kitchen at that time, so we got by alright.

Norwichtown

Kelvin Stott — born 1936
(see page 113)

I was just two when the storm hit, but I remember hearing stories from my parents and grandparents about that hurricane. My parents, Robert Jr. and Grace Stott, lived with my grandparents, Robert Sr. and Mabel Stott, in a two-family house on the Mountain Ash Farm, a 180 acre dairy farm on the top of Plain Hill Road in Norwichtown. It is always windy up here, and in 1938 they really got hit hard.

The Mountain Ash Farm before the storm. The building on the left with the cuploa is the horse barn.
— *Kelvin Stott*

Behind our house stood a dairy barn, a chicken coop, and a horse barn. During the storm, my grandpa Stott went out to the chicken coop. Some of the windows had blown out, and he was in there trying to replace them. It seemed that just as soon as he put one back in, another would blow out. It was getting kind of vicious, so my father went out and told him to come back inside the house. He said, "Those windows are blowing out faster than you can replace them. We'll come back after the storm and put the windows in." My father and grandfather ran back to the house. As they got to the house, which was close by, they turned back around and saw that the chicken coop was not there anymore. The whole building had blown away—just as they were running to the house.

It was September, and they had been haying all summer, so the dairy barn was filled with hay. The top of that barn blew off, but most of the hay was still in place. After the storm, they had to get big tarps to put over the top of the barn and the hay to protect what was left of it.

Shortly before the storm hit, my father and grandfather had bought the farm from my great-grandparents, Joseph and Henrietta Stott. They had paid them everything they had in cash, so they didn't have any money left for insurance. When the storm came, none of the buildings were insured for damage. They had to fix what they could themselves. So when the whole top of the

horse barn blew off, they just went out in the field and took the old roof apart and rebuilt the roof back on the barn board by board—salvaging as much of the material as they could.

The dairy barn was destroyed, but they still wanted to keep dairying, so they gathered up a whole bunch of rocks that were on the property and they started to build back. There was a neighbor down the road who was a good stonemason and carpenter. He helped them rebuild. There was another farm nearby that had a whole bunch of spruce trees—big old spruce trees. When the hurricane came, it knocked all those trees down. Their family was wondering what they to do with all those downed trees. Then someone suggested they get a sawmill, so they did. The very first lumber that went through that sawmill became the framing for the new roof of our dairy barn—from wood that came from spruce trees that were felled in the hurricane. That was the Wilcox sawmill. Eventually they employed thirty people there.

Rebuilding the Stott dairy barn with lumber milled from spruce trees felled in the hurricane.
— *Kelvin Stott*

HURRICANE

State of Emergency Declared Thursday

For three hours after 4 o'clock Wednesday afternoon Norwich was in the grip of a tropical hurricane that left the city and town a scene of appalling destruction when it had blown itself out. The wind came from the east and stripped the Rose of New England of its petals.

All electric power was shut off and the city gas and electric plant was under water so that the city and town were a community with neither light nor electric power through the night. That condition still continues.

STREETS A TANGLED MAZE

Giant trees were ripped up by the roots and fell across the streets all over the city, bringing electric light wires and poles down with them. Practically every street was a jungle of fallen trees and tangled wires which shut off all travel except on foot by dodging around through the maze.

The force of the wind, accompanied by torrents of rain, ripped tin roofs off and carried immense sheets through the air like feathers hanging them up on telegraph poles where they dangled crazily in the air.

FRANKLIN SQUARE AFLOAT

Franklin square was filled with water from the Shetucket rive... rd at the Bath street corner the water was over a ...an's head while the extreme limit of the rise up Franklin street was almost to Willow street. In the Bulletin office the water stood several inches above the window sills.

The Norwich Bulletin,
September 23, 1938.
— from the collection
of Norma Guile
Kornacki

Opposite: the
Frieght House.
— photograph by Ada
R. Chase from the
collection of
Diane A. Norman

The Norwich Bulletin, September 23, 1938

A survey of the damage to buildings in this city
by the storm is as follows:

– Part of the roof of the Werman Shoe Co.'s building was blown off and power supply lines down.

– Roof of the county jail damaged.

– New York, New Haven, and Hartford freight station a total wreck.

– Freight sheds of the Thames River Line collapsed.

– Much of the Lumber of the Dawley Lumber Co. was carried out into the harbor.

– The roof of the Broadway School was blown off and the top floor damaged. Many windows were blown out.

– The roof of Yantic Grain Co. was seriously damaged.

– Roofs of the Central Baptist Church and the Otis Library badly damaged.

The Edward Chappell Company. — *photograph by Ada R. Chase from the collection of Diane A. Norman*

– Part of the roof of the old Masonic Temple was tipped off, as was that of the Breed Theater building and the Broadway theater building.

– United Metal Co. roof damaged as was also the top floor.

– International Silver Co. front wall collapsed

– One tower of the Congregational Church collapsed.

– Steeple of Trinity Episcopal Church toppled.

– Roof of the Beth Jacob Synagogue was ripped off.

– Clock tower of City Hall badly damaged.

– The roofs of Sachem Motor Co. and Norwich Grain Co. were badly damaged.

– The United States Finishing Co. had roofs torn off and much valuable machinery under water.

– Park Congregational Church had large sections of slate ripped off the roof.

– St. Patrick's Church on Broadway had the gold cross blown off its steeple, the slate roof over the main alter ripped off, and stained glass windows on the south side of the church blown in.

– Saxton Woolen Mill at Norwichtown on the Yantic River lost its roof as did the Glen Woolen Mill farther down the stream and the Falls Mill had a large section of the building ripped out.

– The Norwich Dairy Co. and Brownings Dairy made milk deliveries only to families with babies.

– All the plate glass windows of the Woolworth Five & Ten Cent store on Main Street were blown out and also plate glass windows at Plaut Cadden Co. and McAnn's store on Franklin street, The Bulletin Co. lost a plate glass window in the office front and the Goldberg Tire Co. had a window broken.

– A good sized cabin cruiser that had broken loose from its moorings floated up Market Street and ran aground in front of the Auditorium Hotel at the corner of Market and Water Streets.

– The whole of the Central Wharf section between the West Side bridges was under water and boats were used to ferry people between the bridges from Falls Avenue to the new bridge over the east branch of the Yantic River. One young fellow got into his tights and went swimming between the bridges.

Remains of the Freight House.
— *photograph by Edward & Mary Carlson*

– The tower on the old Steiner building on Church Street was toppled over and the large ball on top of the NFA Domestic Science building on Broadway went sailing off and landed on the next lot against the Charles Sexton garage.

– The new Dahl Oil Co. plant on West Main Street was badly damaged and the Chappell Co. building and Charles Lamb's lumber sheds had the roofs gone.

– Laurel Hill Avenue from the bridge to the city line was blocked by fallen trees.

– A large section of the north end of the Ponemah Mills was ripped off, allowing the water to enter the building. A section of one of the roofs in that part of the mill was also ripped off. The large chimney was cracked by the wind and all of the beautiful pine trees in front of the building were snapped roof or uprooted.

– A small section of the roof and wall of the southwest corner of Sacred Heart Church was ripped off.

– A big section of the roof and part of the wall on the south side of the J.B. Martin plant was torn off. The looms and other machinery flooded.

– Jewett City was in shambles. The Finn Block on Main Street was practically demolished. A large portion of the roof of Aspinook plant and two sections of the Ashland Corp. plant were ripped off. The building of the Textile Novelty Co. was practically destroyed.

– The Eighth Street bridge fell into the Shetucket River on Thursday.

– Numerous small buildings, along with telephone poles, railroad ties, chicken coops, dead dogs, and other debris were washed down the Shetucket River.

– Early Wednesday morning as the water from the Shetucket River was rising over old Jewett City River Road at the Blissville flats in Lisbon, a flock of over 100 chickens deserted their coop and flew to the top of the building.

– A long stretch of the Baltic-Taftville highway at the Baltic flats was washed away. A two-decker chicken coop along with an undetermined number of white leghorn chickens owned by the Dupont family floated down the river. The building came to a stop on the westerly side of the highway near the bad curve a short distance south of the Baltic baseball diamond. Members of the family early Thursday afternoon were rescuing chickens from the top story.

Norwich Bulletin

1790 · 1938

VOL. (DAILY EDITION) LXXIX — NORWICH PUBLICATION 34,425 — NORWICH, CONN., MONDAY, SEPTEMBER 26, 1938. — 8 PAGES — CIRCULATION M. AND E. 20,206 WEEK ENDING SEPT. 17 — PRICE TWO CENTS

9 BUILDINGS ARE CONDEMNED

On Bath and Main Streets—Inspections Continuing—Health Orders Issued on Buying in Restricted Area

Nine buildings, wholly or partly, which were badly damaged by the combined flood and hurricane, have been voted condemned and ordered razed by the city emergency inspectors committee, appointed by Acting Mayor Leon P. Lewis and Fire Chief Henry R. Taft, building inspector for Norwich. This action was taken

Czech Manpower Guard Frontiers

Mobilization Has Reached a Stage That the Army Is Ready For Any Emergency

PRAGUE, Sept. 24—(AP)—Czechoslovakia's manpower guarded the frontiers today against any threat to the republic...

FRENCH PREMIER FLIES TO LONDON

Nature of the French Stand Approved by the Cabinet Has Not Been Immediately Disclosed

PARIS, Sept. 24 — (AP) — Premier Edouard Daladier and Foreign Minister Georges Bonnet flew to London today backed by the cabinet's unanimous approval of France's stand on Adolf Hitler's latest demands on Czechoslovakia.

The minister took off at 5:45 a. m. (11:45 p. m. e. s. t. Sunday) in a drenched rain... The cabinet... approved by the cabinet was not immediately disclosed. The communique issued at the end of the cabinet meeting, when Daladier and Bonnet departed, said:

"The cabinet heard expositions of Daladier and Bonnet (Prime Minister Neville Chamberlain by the chancellor of the reich).

"It approved unanimously the..."

Hitler to Speak in Berlin Tomorrow

He Awaits Czech Reply to the Fuehrer's Latest Demands For Ceding Sudetenland

BERLIN, Sept. 25—(AP)—Chancellor Adolf Hitler will speak tomorrow night before a great mass meeting in Berlin Sports palace. The speech will begin at 8 p. m.

Other buildings condemned are the Columbian House, 4 Franklin street; top floor of the Chelsea Lunch building, 212 Main street; Steiner building, 265 Main street, down to the first floor; structure in the rear of the Disco building, formerly occupied by Parker and Preston and the top floor of the apartment house at No. 135 Hill street.

Numerous other buildings inspected by the committee were ordered closed and a placard bearing the inscription "Unfit for Occupancy" was placed on the front entrance.

Sound moving pictures of all buildings inspected are being taken by M. Davis Alexander, architect of Chandler and Palmer, who is chairman of the committee. This is being done, said Chairman Alexander, to support the recommendations of the committee.

Members of the committee on Sunday morning inspected the buildings on Water street, the Boston store, Breed building and Wauregan hotel, and made a survey of the buildings on Main street in the afternoon. Decisions will be made and vote taken on these buildings at another meeting of the committee.

BUY ONLY FROM
APPROVED STORES
IN FLOOD AREA

Dr. Clarence G. Thompson, city health officer, issued the warning Sunday that the people should not buy anything from stores in the flood area until they have been officially placarded with the health approval sign.

The area covered is from Willow to West Main street, Market, Water and Commerce streets, and the Franklin square section.

The official placard reads as follows:

This building has been inspected and may be opened for use. Approved.

Opposite: the Edward Chappell Company.
— *photograph by Ada R. Chase*
from the collection of Diane A. Norman

This page: articles from the *Norwich Bulletin*, September, 26 1938.

51

W1EBO
1930's

NORWICH   CONN.
Radio   QSA   R
Ur sigs wkd hr   QRI   QSB
193 at   M. .S.T.   Band   MC

W1EBO

Transmitter:
Receiver:
Remarks: Portable W1FFI
Pse QSL OM. Tnx.   Woodrow W. Guile   586 Main S

Woodrow W. Guile
and his QSL ham
radio card.
— *Norma Guile
Kornacki*

FAMILIES WEATHER THE STORM

Some families were able to gather together stories of the hurricane from multiple people, offering a broader perspective on the impact of the storm. Below are their stories from Norwich and the surrounding areas.

The Guile Family

Norma Guile Kornacki was born in 1934. Her father, Woodrow W. Guile, born in 1912, played an important role in establishing communication with other communities during and after the storm. Norma shared her own memories, along with a letter written by her father describing his experience during the hurricane.

Norma: I was only four and a half years old at the time. My first recollection of the storm is of my mother, Viola, and my grandmother, Ida, and myself. We were in the city, shopping. It was a short walk from the center of the city to the East Side, where we all lived, on East Main Street, across from Bishops School. You could tell something was coming in the air, but we didn't know what. We had to cross the Preston City Bridge, which was a wooden bridge in those days. I remember the bridge was swaying back and forth in the wind. My mother held my hand with one of hers and with her other hand she was holding onto the railing. My grandmother was ahead of us, and she was holding onto the railing to steady herself against the wind, too. Of course, to me it was fun. I didn't realize the seriousness of it, but my mother was worried that the bridge was going to fall in the water. She was prodding my grandmother to move along so we could get off the bridge as quickly as possible.

We got back home. During the storm, the winds really started picking up. There was an enormous tree in the Bishops School playground that was directly in front of our house. The tree uprooted, and fell right across the street. The upper branches landed on our house, and all the lower branches were piled up around it. My father, Woodrow W. Guile, worked for Norwich Gas & Electric, and he was on call that day. He had to really push against the branches just to get our door open so he could get out and go to work. As he was getting ready to leave for work, we heard this terrific noise upstairs. My parents rushed upstairs, and I followed them. My bedroom was upstairs in the back of the house, and the window in my bedroom had blown in. I had a twin bed right under the window, and now it was covered in glass! I stood there

Article from *QST Amateur Radio* monthly, November 1938, Vol XXII. — *from the collection of Norma Guile Kornacki*

At Norwich, most severely hit inland town, amateur radio proved itself an indispensable adjunct to relief work. At 6 P.M., realizing that a major catastrophe was occurring, Norwich amateurs began to assemble equipment. To obtain emergency power it was necessary to commandeer a gas-driven 300-watt generator from its reluctant owner, with the combined aid of the mayor, National Guard and State Police.

With rare good sense, all Norwich amateurs coöperated in manning one station—W1EBO—high on its hilltop location. In the crew besides W1EBO were W1DET, W1ALW, W1LJX, W1KYV, W1CJN, W1LHF and John Dynon, all but the latter two and W1DET being N.C. Reservists. A 5-meter link using Army equipment relayed to City Hall. Without exception, all communications, official and otherwise, went through this station to W1BDI and W1AW for four days.

crying and asked, "How am I going to go to bed tonight?" I remember my father telling me very calmly, "Don't worry, we will clean it up."

My father left for work, but when the hurricane got real bad, he came back home. He decided to go up to Palmer Street, to his parent's house, and he took my mother, my grandmother, and me along with him, so we wouldn't be alone. His parents, Daniel and Annie Guile, lived at 120 Palmer Street on the East Side. My father was an amateur radio operator (ham). He wanted to go to his parents, because there was an outbuilding by his parent's house that everyone called "The Shack," which was where he kept all of his radio equipment. He had been asked to go and operate the radio equipment in order to provide emergency communication in and out of the city since the city was now completely in silence.

I remember being at my grandmother's house, right across from the shack. From there, I saw the fire chief's car and the police chief's car, and there were several other ham radio operators who gathered there as well. They all knew that was the emergency area. There were quite a few people milling around. That was later in the day after the major part of the storm was over. My father was called on to transmit messages to Hartford for the fire and police.

The following is an account written by Woodrow W. Guile (W1EBO)

"The night of September 21, 1938, the American Red Cross and the wire chief of the local telephone company requested aid in getting in communication with Hartford as all means of communication with the outside were out. Being unable to get into the city, due to fallen trees and debris, it was necessary to wait until daybreak. At 7AM W1ALW rowed into the store where he was employed and succeeded in salvaging eight B batteries. He then got an Army truck and proceeded to W1EBO's (Woodrow W. Guile) home, knowing that he had an SW-3 receiver and transmitter, which could easily be changed to battery operation. From there we went to his shack, which is situated on a high hill overlooking the city and started to work. W1KYV arrived by this time and he was immediately sent out to get more B batteries, which he succeeded in doing. At one time, we had as many as 30 B batteries. At 11AM we were set to go.

Immediately an ORR was sent out. The first to answer was W1DUC in Lebanon, Conn., who had telephone communication into Hartford, Conn. Important messages to the Gov. and Red Cross officials were handled through him until we succeeded in making direct contact with Hartford through W1BDI. As soon as W1AW had power, he had then taken all our traffic (messages).

As there was so much traffic into Norwich, W1AW switched to fone (microphone) for quick service. It was necessary to have the Mayor, the state police, local police, and National Guard confiscate a gasoline driven AC gener-

Woodrow W. Guile and John Clark in the shack.
— *photograph from the "QST Amateur Radio" monthly, November 1938, Vol XXII from the collection of Norma Guile Kornacki*

ator from a local "patriotic citizen". This simplified matters considerably, as W1DET kindly loaned us his RME69 and we also were able to have lights for night time operation. The transmitter has continued to operate on B batteries as the generator had a capacity of only 300 watts. Filament current was obtained from storage batteries loaned by the National Guard. The drain (on the batteries) being quite high, it was necessary to change batteries often. W1LHF, who was a former Coast Guard operator, served as relief operator Thursday night until 3AM Friday morning. The National Guard kindly loaned us their 5-meter transceivers which were used between the Red Cross headquarters and the radio station, these being operated by a National Guardsman and W1LJX and W1CJN also assisted in the operation of the station. John Dynon and Stanley Scraba were kindly loaned by the city of Norwich Gas & Electric Department who did a fine job of typing and filing the messages that were received and transmitted.

All of these men with the exception of, W1DET, John Dynon and Stanley Scraba are members of the N.C.R. (Navel Communication Reserves). Food and coffee were kindly furnished by the Red Cross. At 8PM September 26, it was decided that an emergency no longer existed and the men went home for a well earned rest. See you in the next hurricane!"

The Buckley Family

Ruth (Buckley) Sanders was born in 1930. She and her brothers, Robert Buckley, born in 1933, and Richard (Dick) Buckley, born in 1922, lived in the Falls area of Norwich on Williams Street.

Ruth: I was eight years old, and I happened to be home sick from school that day. The weather started to get very windy. My mother, Ann, began to get worried because my brother, Robert, who wasn't even five years old, was in kindergarten at the Falls School over on Sachem Street. The wind was really blowing, so she decided to go up to the school to get him. My mother walked up Williams Street and down Oneco Street to the school. When she got there, she found out the children had already been dismissed. My brother had left with Betty Dahl, who lived up the street from us. They must have taken the other way around the block and missed my mother. I was watching out a window of our house, when I saw my brother and Betty walking back. Suddenly, I saw Betty's aunt, who lived across the street from us, run out into the street and grab the two of them. She ran them back to her house. The three of them just about made it onto her porch when a big part of a tree fell right in the spot where they had just been standing. Right as the tree fell, I saw my mother coming back around the corner. She ran across the street and grabbed my brother from the porch, and then turned and ran back home with him.

The Buckley home on Williams Street.
— *Ruth Sanders*

Robert: I remember when my mom grabbed me and we ran across the street. When we got back into our house, our mother told us we all had to stay in the hallway. She thought that was the safest part of the house, because of all of the walls there.

Our father, William, was the foreman at the Dawley Lumber Company, down by the Thames River. During the storm, he was watching the water come up. When it got pretty high, he went in to see Mr. Dawley. He told him he was afraid the lumber was going to be washed out and said they should start moving it away from the river. Mr. Dawley said, "Don't worry about it. It'll be OK." So my father left the office, but just as he started walking away, he saw all the lumber starting to float down the river. My father turned around and went back into the office and told Mr. Dawley what was happening. The water was coming up so fast by then that Mr. Dawley told him, "Bill, you better get everyone out of here! I'm leaving too." They all ran out of there fast.

H. F. & A. J. Dawley

MANUFACTURERS, WHOLESALE AND RETAIL DEALERS IN

Lumber, Yellow Pine, Shingles, Nails, Windows, Doors, Lime, Cement, Etc.

Telephones 62—63

Office and Yard at New Dock   Planing Mill at Fort Point

Laurel Hill Avenue   Norwich, Conn.

Ruth: Our brother Fred was at Dawley's with my father that day. When they were coming home, they could only get as far as Chelsea Bank. They ended up going around and coming up Broadway. As they went by the Broadway School, they saw the slates were starting to blow off the roof of the school. They said they were flying off the roof—like you would throw a frisbee. They were flying every which way, across the street, and right into people's windows. My father and brother had a hard time getting back to our house with all that going on, and they weren't even that far away from our home.

> The slates were flying right off the roof, just like you would throw a frisbee. They were flying every which way across the street and right into people's windows.

Later after the storm, my father and Fred went back down to Dawley's. They were pulling whatever lumber out of the Thames River that they could salvage. I remember my mother was mad at my father for having my brother work down there in that water.

At some point during the storm, we heard a great big *bang*. It was so loud, we thought the roof of our house had come off. We were lucky. A tree had fallen on our roof, but it didn't do much damage—only a few shingles needed to be replaced.

Dick: That tree was just leaning up against our house. It didn't hurt the roof too much. It was just laying there on it. The city came and took that tree down. There was another one that fell and ruined the sidewalk, but they said it was still alive and they were going to leave it there. Later, we went out and made a cut all the way around the bark on that tree so it would die, so then the city had to come and take it away.

I wasn't home during the storm. Earl Potter was a teacher at Norwich Free Academy where he taught bookkeeping and typing. He was a friend of our family, and he lived on the corner of Uncas and Sachem Streets in a house along with a few other teachers. It had been a pretty nice

Graduation on the Campus, June 1938

morning. Earl had asked us if we wanted to go swimming after school, so when school got out at 1:30, a few of us drove down to Eastern Beach in Groton.

We weren't there too long when the weather started to get a little rough. We saw a small tree fall down near us, but we still hadn't heard anything about any storm yet. Earl said we had better start heading home. As we started driving back, we got across the New London Bridge but were stopped at the Coast Guard Academy where a guard told us that this was a hurricane. We continued trying to get home. At that time, you had to drive right through the campus of Connecticut College to get to Norwich. The bypass road hadn't been built yet. I remember those college girls were out running around outside, as slates were flying off the roofs of the buildings. We kept driving towards home. There were trees down all over the place. At one point we got behind this big truck. The driver called out to us, "Follow me, I'll get through one way or the other." So we did. We got to a place where there was a great big tree across the road. The truck driver said the only way we could get by was to cut across some guy's yard. I remember the guy came out and was yelling like anything at us. He was so angry that this big truck was tearing up his yard and making a mess of it. We got up to Norwich—as far as Asylum Street. The bridge was

Opposite top: graduation at NFA in June 1938, three months before the storm.

Opposite bottom: view of the same hillside taken after the hurricane.

Above: the NFA football team clearing away trees on the bleachers.

— photographs from NFA Mirror, 1940

59

out, but the footbridge over the railroad tracks was still there. So we parked on Asylum Street and walked across the footbridge to get home. That was a long drive back. It was probably about 3 o'clock in the morning when I finally got home.

Robert: The next day, me, my father, and Fred went out and walked over to Mikutel's, our local grocery store, on the corner of Sachem and Oneco Street. I remember just trying to get to the store with all those trees down was a real challenge, especially for me. I was so small that my father and brother had to keep helping me up and over the big tree trunks. We had brought some gunnysacks—you know, the cloth sacks that grain used to come in. When we got to the store, we bought all the canned goods that we could fit in those sacks. We came back home with two great big sacks full of canned foods. We had lost electricity, and we knew the canned food wouldn't spoil.

Dick: I was on the NFA football team. A few days after the storm we had football practice, but what the team ended up doing for "practice" was cleaning up the campus after the storm. We cut up all the big trees that fell down on the field. Of course we just had hand saws, so it took us a while. It was a real mess out there. The trees fell right on top of the bleachers, and flattened them all out.

The Banas and Planeta Families

Betty (Banas) Wisniewski, born 1921, lived with her mother on Sachem Street, right around the corner from the Buckley family. Betty's niece, Irene (Planeta) Algiers, born 1930, lived in an apartment downstairs from her.

Betty: I lived on Sachem Street with my mother, Anna Banas. My mother owned the building with an A&P store below and several apartments above and behind the store. My mother and I lived upstairs. I used to work for Mrs. Leary, a woman up the street. Her husband worked on the postal train and was away from home every other week, so when he was away, I would stay with her for the whole week and help her around the house or help her children with their homework. The Learys paid me three dollars for each week I worked, plus room and board. The week of the storm was one of the weeks I was working for Mrs. Leary.

On the day of the hurricane, I went to school at NFA and then headed over to Mrs. Leary's house through the pouring rain. No one was there, so I let myself in and started vacuuming. The vacuum stopped, and at first I was afraid I had broken her vacuum, but pretty soon I realized the power had been knocked out by the storm. Then I heard water coming in from the window in their dining room. I had to go outside to fix the screen on the window. I took a chair outside to stand on so I could reach the window. I got the screen back in, but then a big wind came and blew me off the chair. I got up, went inside, and started mopping up the water on the dining room floor. Finally, Mrs. Leary came home. She said a tree had just missed falling on her on her way home. It just missed her.

I stayed the night with them. The next morning we still really didn't know just how bad the storm was. I made myself lunch and headed out to school. Someone stopped me on the street and said, "Where do you think you're going? The schools aren't open today." So I started to head back to my home, but there was no road! I couldn't see the street. All of the large trees that had been on each side of our street were now down lying across the street. I had to climb over them. When I got to the A&P, I saw

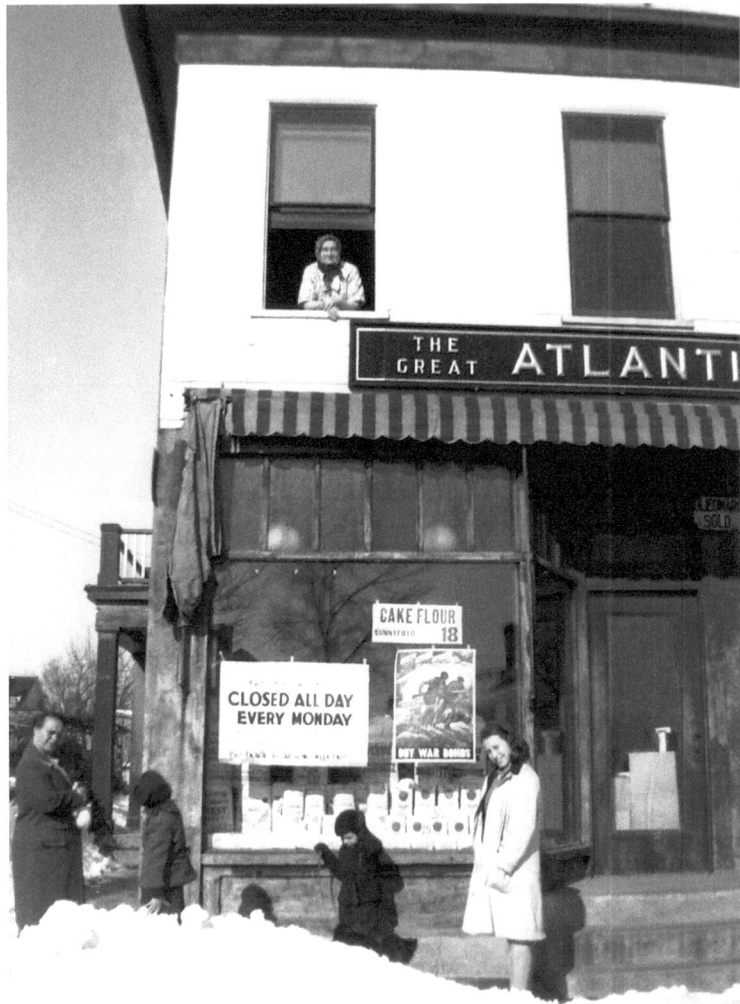

The A&P on Sachem Street in the 1940s. Anna Banas is in the window. Irene Planeta is on the sidewalk on the right, Caroline Planeta is on the left.
— *Betty Wisniewski*

the front window of the store had been knocked out by the wind. My brother-in-law, John Planeta, had boarded it up. My mother was so happy to see me. There had been no way for her to contact me. She had been praying all night that the Leary's house was still standing. During the storm, she had seen a house on the corner of Lafayette Street and Sherman blow right over and fall down the valley across the street. Later we learned that the whole third floor of the Falls Mill had blown off. That was just down the hill from us, and my parents used to work there.

Irene: I was eight and a half years old and in the third grade at the Falls School, which was right next door to our house. Normally, we got out of school at 3:20 in the afternoon, but that day our

Above and opposite: Sachem Street. The Uncas Monument is visible on right in the photograph above. — *both photographs by Ada R. Chase from the collection of Diane A. Norman*

principal, Miss Hayes, came in and whispered something to our teacher, Miss Ahern, who then turned and told us that we were dismissed and we were to go immediately home. I didn't have far to go, but, oh boy, the wind was whipping and the rain was pouring down.

Once I was home, we heard a loud noise. A tree had crashed down on the top of the Gwudz's house up the street. Some windows on our property had been blown in by the storm. I was outside watching Mr. Stephaniak, who lived upstairs from us. He was putting up boards over the windows. His eleven-year-old son, Martin Jr., tried to help. He picked up a piece of plywood, but then the wind picked him and the board up like a sail and carried him several feet off the ground. Mr. Stephaniak thought his son was fooling around and gave him a whack for picking up the board. Just then the wind knocked me right over. I think everyone began to realize that the storm was getting really bad. In the play yard of the Falls School there had been a huge tree that had orange flowers in the spring. That tree crashed down on the school's bell tower and knocked it down. They never put that bell back. Instead, they replaced it with an electric bell. I always missed the *ding-dong* sound of that old bell.

Meanwhile back in our house, my grandmother, Anna Banas, kept running around lighting holy candles. She thought since they were holy, they would protect us in the storm. My mother, Caroline Planeta, was afraid the candles would start a fire, so she kept running around blowing them out, but then my grandmother would go and light them again... I think my mother and grandmother fought about the candles throughout the whole storm! My mother kept pulling everyone away from the windows. She was afraid they might blow in.

Across the street from us was there was a young couple who lived in a little cottage. Their house was right on the edge of a ravine that went down toward the Falls Mill. There was a set of steps there that you could use as a shortcut from Sachem Street down to the lower part of Yantic Street. As I was looking out of my parents' bedroom window at their cottage, I saw it tilt a little, then a little more, and then it just toppled over and disappeared down the ravine!

My father was working at J.B. Martin. He had gotten out at 3 o'clock and tried to drive home, but he had to abandon his car by the Broadway Theater. All the downed trees made the road impassable. He had to walk all the way home. My mother was so very worried about him. He got back very late at night—drenched and dirty. It's a wonder he made it home at all. He said he had to crawl under the fallen trees, because each time he tried to crawl over them the wind just knocked him down. He said there were a few times when the wind was really bad that the safest thing he could do was just hide under trees.

The next day was gorgeous. My aunt, Betty (Banas), came home from where she had been working overnight. The two of us walked down to Chelsea Parade climbing over all the trees. There were so many trees in the street—and roofs, too. When we got to the park, all the beautiful big elm trees were gone. There had been a tree about every hundred feet along the park and there were benches under them. Families with young children and older people used to go and sit and relax in the cool of the trees. Now they were all gone!

When school started up again, some of the kids from the Broadway School, which had been damaged, were sent over to join our third and fourth grades. We had those old desks and chairs that were screwed to the floor, and there weren't enough desks for everyone, so we had to double

up and share seats—rear end to rear end—one facing front and one facing the desk behind. Most of our desks had two children at them.

The Bargnesi and Cormier Families

Dan Bargnesi was born in 1932. His family lived up on Jail Hill. His cousin, Terri (Cormier) Homiski and her family lived next door. Although she was born six weeks after the hurricane, her parents had told her about the hurricane so many times that she can tell their story for them.

Dan: I was in the first grade at St. Patrick School. All of a sudden the wind started blowing like crazy. All of us kids were getting scared and were looking all around. I remember the nun got upset with us, because she wanted us to quiet down and behave. All of a sudden we heard a big *snap!* There was a huge evergreen tree in the backyard of the school, and it just snapped and fell over. That made the nun worried, so she grabbed us and took us down to the basement of the school. We weren't down there too long when I saw Uncle Pete Tombari (who was actually my cousin) come to pick up his daughters, Joanne and Teresa. He saw me and told the nun, "That's my nephew. I can take him home." We lived up on Cedar Street. Normally, to get to our house you would go right up Slater Avenue and take a left onto Cedar, and it would take about five minutes. That day we couldn't go on Slater Avenue. Instead, we had to go up to Broadway and then down Washington Street all the way to Washington Square. There were so many trees down and so many fires

> I heard a loud snap above me. I looked up and saw this big branch falling out of the tree. I just froze where I was and started screaming.

from the downed power lines that we couldn't get through any other way. Uncle Pete stopped over by his house, and he said to me, "OK now, run home!" There I am, five years old, and I was running like hell! I got a short way up my street and I heard a loud *snap* above me. I looked up and saw this big branch falling out of the tree. I just froze where I was and started screaming. The branch fell all around me, but somehow it didn't touch me, not even one leaf. I was left standing there with the tree all around me. One of the Ciccone boys was in his doorway looking out and he saw me. He ran across the street, grabbed me, and carried me to my house. I was just a skinny little kid then; I probably weighed about forty pounds. We lived on the first floor of our house and my Nonna, Nunziatta (Nancy) Leone, lived upstairs. There was a set of outside stairs that led to the second floor where my grandparents lived. By the time I got home, those steps had already blown down right in front of our door.

My younger sister Jean, who was two and a half at the time, was home with my mother, Mariette, and the new baby, Jackie. We were all going from one room to the other—back and forth. In our living room, we had those old-fashioned carpets on the wooden floor. It was an old house and the wind of the storm was getting in, making the carpets float up. Jean and I were sitting there on the sofa and watching the carpets float up in the air. We had fun watching them go up and down, and up and down... Then we went into my bedroom in the back of the house. From there, I remember looking at my Aunt Lucy's house and seeing the shingles flying off of it—one at a time. I went and told my mother, "Momma, Aunt Lucy's roof is peeling off!" My mother just looked at me and said, "Stop it. Get out of here and go sit somewhere quiet." So I went back to my bedroom and I looked back out the window. Aunt Lucy's whole roof was gone! I could look right down inside their house through the open rafters. I ran back and told my mother, "Aunt Lucy's roof is gone!" That's when my mother really got upset, especially since my Aunt Lucy was very pregnant at the time.

My father, Louis Bargnesi, was working over on Laurel Hill at the Thermos. He was on the 3 to 11 o'clock shift that day. They didn't let him out until about 9 o'clock at night. By then the storm had already gotten real bad and it was dark. He tried to get home, but he wasn't allowed over the Laurel Hill Bridge. They had it blocked, so he had to walk all the home. Of course, my mother was panicked. It was about probably about 3 o'clock in the morning by the time he got home. I think he walked up through Greeneville. I remember he said it was scary being out there in the dark with the downed trees and wires all over the place.

My mother tried to put us to sleep that night, but we couldn't sleep. That wind was so loud. I can still hear that wind in my head today. I remember staring at the walls of my room worried about them blowing in.

The next day, there was the weirdest yellow sky I have ever seen. There was no rain, but there were still clouds and they were a strange yellow-greenish color. My mother, sweet Mariette, saw all of the young guys outside working, trying to clear the wires and branches. She boiled big pots of water on an old wood stove we had and made hot coffee for all of them, serving them out of our garage.

Terri: I was born November 1, 1938, just about six weeks after the Hurricane of 1938. I remember my mother, Lucy Cormier, describing the day of the storm to me. Around mid-morning the weather began to get very gray, cloudy, and ominous looking. The wind started to pick up and quickly caught my mother's attention. My family lived in a small two-story cape at 42 Cedar Street in Norwich, not too far away from City Hall, and my mother's parents lived right next door to us. During the storm, my grandmother came over to make sure that my mother was alright. She was very worried, because my mother was seven and a half months pregnant with me at the time.

When my grandmother got to our house, she heard a thunderous noise. The house was being hit hard by the storm from the front. My grandmother found my mother in the living room—terrified. She was screaming that windows are going to blow in. My grandmother grabbed her to get her out of there. As they left to run into the kitchen, the living room door slammed shut behind them. Seconds later the two front windows blew in. Within minutes of the windows blowing in, my mother and grandmother heard a noise so loud and ear shattering that they thought it was the end of the world. The peak of the roof of the house was just above the living room windows facing Cedar Street. That noise they heard was the entire roof being lifted off of the house in one piece. They thought it must have happened due to the air pressure in that room changing after the door had slammed shut. The roof landed in the back yard—in ONE piece. My cousin, Dan, who was five and a half years old, was living next door in my grandparents' apartment at that time. He looked out of his window and saw the roof had blown off my mother's house. He ran and told his mom, "Aunt Lucy's roof is gone!"

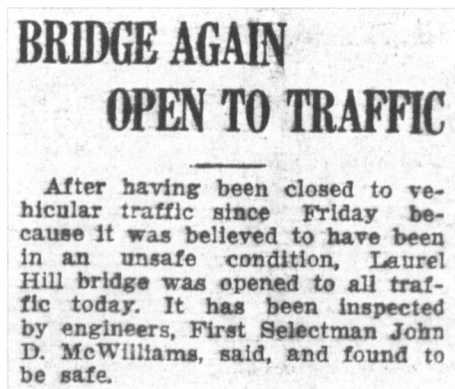

BRIDGE AGAIN OPEN TO TRAFFIC

After having been closed to vehicular traffic since Friday because it was believed to have been in an unsafe condition, Laurel Hill bridge was opened to all traffic today. It has been inspected by engineers, First Selectman John D. McWilliams, said, and found to be safe.

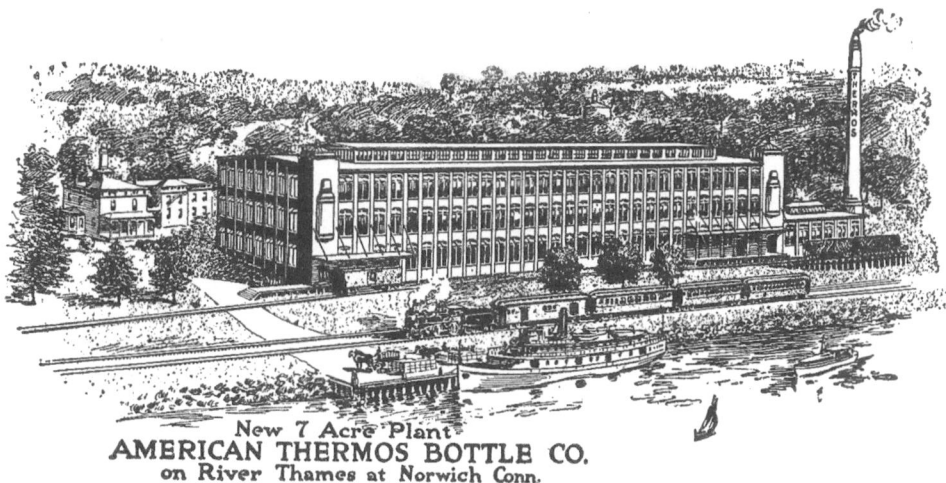

THERMOS

New 7 Acre Plant
AMERICAN THERMOS BOTTLE CO.
on River Thames at Norwich Conn.

My grandmother and mother went down into the cellar. There was a small door down there that led to the house next door, which was owned by a woman named Nellie Fitzgerald. Nellie's house was a beautiful two-story brick building with an apartment under the main house. My grandmother and mother crawled on their hands and knees through a dirt tunnel from their cellar to the neighbor's. My mother crawled even though she was seven and a half months pregnant with me! Years later I did some research about the Jail Hill area where we lived. I learned that area used to be part of the Underground Railroad that helped slaves escape to the North. That tunnel that my mom and grandmother had crawled through during the storm was one of the tunnels that had been used by the Underground Railroad.

My father, Len Cormier, was at work at the Thermos over on Laurel Hill. He had to leave the Thermos on foot during the storm. He walked to the city, stepping and crawling over all of the downed power lines and the beautiful trees that had fallen along Laurel Hill. He said the trees looked like a bunch of wooden matchsticks had been thrown up in the air and fallen down in the streets. His biggest fear was of all the power lines that were tangled in and around many of the trees that he had to walk over. Luckily the Laurel Hill Bridge wasn't out yet, so he was able to make it up Broadway to get over near the Courthouse. He decided to crawl up the steep wooded area behind the Central Baptist Church, which brought him to the lots directly across the street from our house. The lots were a big area where we used to go sliding and played baseball as kids. When he got up there, he stood looking down on our house. It was standing there as it always had… only minus its entire roof!

My father he couldn't find my mother inside our home, so he began going from house to house looking for her. When he finally found her, I'm sure that they had a tearful reunion.

I know my mother never truly got over that storm. For the rest of her life, whenever she heard the wind start to kick up, she had my father board up all of the windows in our house—top and bottom. Even sixty years after that hurricane, whenever the wind would pick up or when a storm of any kind was forecasted, my mother would get very nervous. She always felt better knowing we were with her.

The Gemino Family

The Gemino family lived on Fountain Street in Norwich. There were six girls in the family, and they all attended Broadway School in September 1938. Five of them tell their memories below, starting with Edna (Gemino) Casper, the eldest of the six girls.

Edna (Gemino) Casper: I was in eighth grade at Broadway School. The roof blew off of our school, and the school was closed for so long that we had to be bussed to the Elizabeth Street School, where I graduated eighth grade. We had always walked to school, so riding the bus was a big deal for us.

When my sisters and I were all safe at home, my momma, Clara, thought it would be a good idea for us to go a few doors down to my grandmother's house. That was until we saw her porch blow off. Then we saw our neighbor's fence across the street flew right up into the air! Our bedroom windows all broke during the storm, and my father, Raffaele, had to put boards over all of them.

Luckily, we had two propane stoves, so momma could still cook. I don't actually recall how long we were without power. We used an old icebox as a

backup to our refrigerator. We had an entire cellar full of canned goods that momma had put up. We ate peaches, plums, and way too much homemade applesauce. To this day, I still don't like applesauce! Bread was rationed, and we were only allowed one slice per person, per day. The meat we ate was from the chickens and rabbits we raised in the backyard. To supplement our food after the storm, my father caught crows in our yard. He rigged up trap by attaching a heavy string to a screen. Then he sprinkled bread crumbs on the ground to lure the crows. He watched the trap from an upstairs window in our house, and when he saw that the time was right, he dropped the screen onto the crows, and then ran outside to get them. He often caught three or four at a time! My momma cleaned the birds and cooked them for us. They tasted good. My sisters and I couldn't really tell they were crows, but then again, my mother was such a great cook. The crows didn't provide much meat, but they did help us get through the days after the storm. We managed until things got back to normal.

The flooding downtown was so devastating that the basements of many of the businesses, such as Woolworths and the Metropolitan, were underwater. They ended up having sales of whatever merchandise they were able to salvage. I recall being able to buy socks for a mere five cents per pair.

Above: the Metropolitan Store in Franklin Square.
— *photograph by Edward & Mary Carlson*

Opposite: looking up Bath Street.
— *photograph by Edward & Mary Carlson*

Dorothy (Gemino) Weady: (submitted by her daughter, Marcia Brennan) I remember my mother saying she was eleven years old at the time. The roof of her school had blown off and they had to attend a different school after the storm. She recalled that the walk home that day was pretty scary, the wind and the rain blowing so hard that the rain was going sideways.

Ruth (Gemino) Troxell: I was seven years old when the hurricane arrived. We all went to the Broadway Elementary School, which was a large red brick building. I was in Miss Duttton's second grade, and, when the weather got bad, Miss Duttton excused us from classes and said we should head home. Before we left the building, we were advised more than once to stay away from broken branches and to be especially careful of any wires on the ground.

Back at our home, we were fortunate not to have had too much damage. A window upstairs smashed in and a few shingles flew off the house. My grandmother, who lived next door, wasn't as lucky. The roof of her house flew right off!

Our school was badly damaged in the storm. Afterwards we had to meet at a school on Laurel Hill. We were instructed to bring a can of soup for lunch every day since we could no longer walk home for lunch like we used to when we went to Broadway.

Elaine (Gemino) Rose: I was five years old, and I remember well the Hurricane of '38. I was upstairs in Poppa's room when the window in his room broke. My mother called me down to the basement, where we all huddled, safe from the storm. There she made us sandwiches of bread and jelly. They were so good, but then again everything she made for us was good.

Shirley (Gemino) Sukut: The only thing I remember was my mother rocking me. I was only two years old at that time. I know as I got older, whenever we had storms, my mom had us kneel down in front of this little white alter with candles, and we would all pray. Whenever the thunder and lightening would made a loud sound, my mom always blessed herself and shouted out, "Oh Jesus, save us!"

The Wight Family

Ruth (Wight) Still was born in 1914. Her family lived on a farm in Sprague. She and her father, Howard Wight, both worked in Norwich. Her brother, Myron Wight, born in 1920, told his memories of the hurricane to his granddaughter, Elizabeth Tefft, in an interview several years ago. Excerpts of his interview are included below along with Ruth's story.

Ruth: I was in Norwich working for Pat McWilliams in his office on West Main Street. He was a general contractor, and I was his typist and general office clerk. My father, Howard Wight, worked for Mr. McWilliams in his wood shop. That business, like many others, was still recovering from the Depression. There wasn't much work, so my father wasn't working full time. He just worked odd hours. My father had brought me in to work in Norwich that morning, but then he left to go back to our farm in Sprague before the storm really got bad. Our office was directly across from the marina, near the A&P store on the corner of Falls Avenue. We were in a strong brick building and none of us realized the severity of the storm yet, so I stayed and worked along with my supervisor, Frank Davis, throughout the storm.

At some point the storm let up a bit, and my supervisor decided we should walk up to his house. Frank's wife had passed away sometime earlier, but he had a live-in housekeeper at his home, so he thought it was best that I should spend the night there rather than trying to go home. There was no way to contact my family, but we thought my father would think to look there to find me. Mr. Davis lived on the far end of West Main Street. The streets were completely

71

Above and right:
storm damage on
the Wight Farm in
Sprague, Conn.
— *Myron Wight*

littered with downed wires, telephone poles, trees, parts of buildings, and all manner of debris. There was absolutely no clear path for us to walk. Sometimes, when I think of all the downed wires, I wonder why we weren't electrocuted that day. Frank Davis was in his late sixties, maybe nearly seventy, and he wasn't in the best of health. It's a miracle he didn't have a heart attack, because even I, at twenty-four years old, had a hard time getting through the mess. It was a strenuous walk. It's hard to believe how much damage was done in such a short amount of time.

Meanwhile, back on the Wight farm in Sprague…

Myron: I was eighteen years old. The weather had been quite wet that whole summer, and in September there was some flooding. The day of the hurricane was very cloudy. The sky was heavily overcast, and it was very humid that morning. In the middle of the morning the wind began to blow. It wasn't anything unusual, so my father and I, and Clarence Still (my sister Ruth's fiancé) went into the woods to cut wood. My father worked in a shop in Norwich, but the shop had been flooded by the river, so he was home from work that day. We were working within calling distance of the house. That was how we generally communicated with each other, by hollering to one another. It was easier than going to find someone. Shortly after noontime,

my mother, who was alone in the house, called out for us to come inside. We knew something must have happened or she wouldn't have called us, so we hurried home. She said there had been a fire in the wood stove and the chimney had caught fire, but by the time we got there, the fire had already gone out. Then we started to notice that the wind was blowing harder than normal for a regular storm. I remember along the edge of the mowing field we had a lot of ash trees. They seemed to bend before the wind, the way bending grass does. The trees would all bend together and then let up again. That seemed quite unusual.

It started to rain, so we decided not to go back out into the woods. We had no communication with the outside. The radio we had wasn't always dependable, depending on how charged the battery was, so we probably didn't have the radio on. That meant we didn't know anything about the weather conditions, except what was going on right there on the top of the hill. We stayed in the house as the winds picked up. There was one window in the ell of the house that faced southeast, the direction the wind was blowing from. That window blew out, but that was no big problem. We just put it back in and nailed it more securely. We didn't think anymore about it. By that point, it was raining hard enough that we didn't want to be outside. The biggest concern for my mother was that the water began to leak in and around the windows. She was very particular about these things and she kept getting old clothes to mop up around the walls and the edges of the windows. I guess the wind got strong enough that my father persuaded her

Hurricane of Sept. 21, 1938

At 3:30 in the afternoon of that fatal autumn day the wind began to blow from the southeast with unusual velocity. In two hours time years of work was destroyed and our hundred acres of timber was turned into a jumble of roots, interlinking tops, and crisscross logs.

Our barn was totally ruined but a goat, a calf, and a bull escaped injury. Sections of roof and side walls were strewn about for a distance of 300 ft. An oak sill 30 ft. long and 10 in. square was blown 100 ft. and some of the rafters were driven 3 or 4 feet into the ground.

All the small buildings were rolled over and the ell on the house was pushed six feet off its foundation. An ash can which was in the rear of the house disappeared entirely.

The following photos give proof of the great strength of the wind.

not to stand near the windows. He was afraid they would blow out. The storm was becoming more serious than anything we had ever experienced before and anything my parents had ever experienced before, too.

At some point we went down to the cellar. My father insisted that we stay on the south side of the cellar. He thought that was the safest place in case the house was blown down. There were only a few small windows down there. It was quite dark, although we may have had a kerosene lantern. My first feeling of fear was of the way the wind blew. We couldn't see outside down there. All we could do was hear the storm. The only way I can explain what it sounded like was a constant roar—like a train. As the storm continued, it got louder. We could hardly speak to each other. We couldn't make our voices loud enough to be heard when the wind hit that high pitch. Each time the wind hit the house, it began to shake. Then almost as quickly as it came, it abated. We couldn't hear anything then, it was almost completely silent. Then in the distance we would hear this sound again. It started small and then built up, and up, and up... to a high pitch again and then died down again.

Once while Clarence and my father were looking out one of the basement windows they saw our barn collapse. They said that the barn fell as if it had been a cardboard box. First the roof lifted up, like you would open the cover of cardboard box, and as it lifted, it carried the walls right along with it. The whole thing flew up in the air and disintegrated into pieces.

At one point, my father thought the storm had reached a low point. He said it would be safer for us to get off the top of the hill. When we came out of the basement, the wind was still blowing strongly. We were having difficulty standing up. The only way we could move was to hold on to each other. Clarence, my father, and I took axes and saws with us, and we headed down the hill to where our car was parked.

Our first thought was that we wanted to get to Norwich. My sister was working in an office there, and she had stayed at work. We had no idea what had happened to her. We decided to take the road to Hanover, because looking down the road by the paper mill, it seemed to be lined with trees which had blown down. We didn't get far when we came across a huge maple tree, about three feet in diameter, directly across the road. The tree was larger than we could cut using the tools we had with us. Even if we could have cut through it, we would have had to then move it by hand. The fields were muddy, making it impossible to drive through them, so we decided to go back another way. We used our axes and saws to cut a path through the trees. When we had left the house, it was about 3 o'clock in the afternoon. By the time we had cut through the maple trees, it was nearly dark.

I'm not exactly sure how, but we did eventually get to Norwich. I believe we had to make a lot of detours. My grandmother, Mary Wuttkey, lived on Roath Street in Norwich, and we managed to get to her house. Most every street in Norwich was blocked. We decided the only way to locate my sister would be to walk down into Norwich and see what happened. What we saw was beyond my comprehension. Living out in the country, we were used to it being dark at night, but I had never seen a city, like Norwich, that was completely dark. It was absolutely black—there were no lights, not even many candles. We only had one flashlight, but we didn't want to use it too much because we didn't have replacement batteries. We tried to walk down to Franklin Square, but we had to make a detour around it. The whole area was completely flooded. When we got down to the part of the city where my sister worked, we saw that there hadn't been any damage to her building. We found a message they had left on the door saying that my sister had gone home with Frank Davis, who lived over on West Main Street. We weren't able to make contact with her until the next day.

Ruth: The next day it was absolutely gorgeous—bright blue sky, no wind. Late that day my family found where I was, and we were all finally reconnected again. After the storm, the office I worked in had to be vacated. They relocated over to the Carroll Building on Main Street.

Myron: We came directly home after we found my sister. We knew there was a lot of work to do. When we got home, the first thing we noticed was that all the trees were completely bare. It went from an atmosphere of summer to one of winter in one day. There weren't even any leaves on the ground—they were either blown away or pulverized. We had recently painted the side of our house that faced southeast. During the storm, leaves had embedded themselves in the paint. The whole side of the house had imprints of all different kinds of leaves.

Our barn had blown away almost completely. I had a pet goat that had been tied up on a chain in the barn. After the storm, she was still there where we left her. The barn was gone, but the goat was still there. We also had a bushel basket in the barn with a cat and a new litter of kittens. They were gone too and when we went to look for them, we found them about five hundred feet from the barn. Believe it or not, the cat and her kittens were still in the basket. We're not sure if they made the trip in the basket or they found the basket again later on their own.

There was an ell, about eight feet wide and twenty feet long, on the back of our house that had been blown off its foundation and tilted up. One of our main projects was to get that back on the foundation. There wasn't much damage to our house, but there was a lot of cleaning to do. Everything was soaking wet. There was so much rain and, because of the way the wind blew, water got in everywhere—through every crack and crevice. Everything had to be dried out and with the high humidity, even things that didn't really get wet still needed to be aired out in the sun—mattresses and everything.

The Wisniewski and Piechowski Families

Gertie (Kotkofski) Wisnieski was born in 1912. She is 101 years old and still has very clear memories of the hurricane. The stories below include several members of her extended family both in Norwich and out on the Wisniewski family farm in Preston.

Gertie: My husband, Joe, and our two daughters, Dorothy and Joan, were living at 5 Rock Street down the hill from the Preston Bridge. We lived in a first-floor apartment very close to the river. There had been a heavy rain that day, and it just kept raining and raining… As the storm went on, the river by our house started to rise. Then, during the storm, there was a tidal wave.

That wave came in so fast that we had to leave our apartment in a hurry. We went up to Fowler Avenue. We knew someone who lived there in a second-floor apartment, and they let us stay with them to take shelter away from the rising waters.

Later when I went back to our apartment, I could see how high the water had come up from the water line on the walls. I had a cross hanging on the wall in our bedroom and I could see that the water had come all the way up to Jesus's feet on that cross. I still have that cross today. We lost pretty much everything. I kept all my dishes and my silverware. My laundry, oh my laundry! All my bureau drawers were full and I had to take all my laundry—my clothes and my linens—and wash everything. I tried to save whatever I could, the little that wasn't ruined. You see, we were newly married, and everything we had was practically new. We only managed to save a few pieces of furniture. We were able to keep our dinning room set, and our bedroom set, although we had to throw out the mattresses. There were a few photos, like the one of Joe and me on our wedding day, that were hanging high enough on the walls that they didn't get damaged. I saved my curtains, although I had to wash them real good. We lost everything else to the storm. Later the Red Cross came and took the rest of the things in our home and just dumped them. We had no flood insurance to help replace any of our possessions.

My husband, Joe, had been at work at the Mohican Market at 262 Main Street in Franklin Square when the storm hit. He was unable to get home, so he had to stay there for three days straight. The first floor of the market had been flooded. However, upstairs where the bakery was located, was still alright. He, along with some other people who worked at the store, slept upstairs on the floor of the bakery for a few days. The Mohican Market was one of the only stores in that area open after the storm. Since their bakery was still intact, they were one of the few bakeries that were still able to make bread. In the wake of the storm

The wedding photograph Gertie and Joe saved from their flooded apartment on Rock Street.
— *Gertie Wisnieski*

Franklin Square (Dr. Solomon is on the left). — *photograph by Edward & Mary Carlson*

they baked extra bread for Willimantic and many other neighboring towns that had been badly hit. Our family couldn't stay in our apartment anymore, so we ended up moving in with my husband's sister, Mary Piechowski, at her home on Commodore Street in Norwich. We stayed with them that whole winter until we got back on our feet again. Then, in April 1939, we bought this place of our own, here on Fanning Avenue.

Dorothy (Wisnieski) Gravel (Gertie's daughter) — born 1934: We lived in a ground floor apartment at 5 Rock Street on the East Side. I remember that my younger sister, Joan, and I were out in the yard when a tree fell down right behind us. When my mother saw that, she was frantic! Our house was one of the lowest ones on the street. We were very close to the water. As the water in the river rose up, we had to move up the hill to a house on Fowler Avenue. All of us who lived there on the bottom by the river had to move from house to house.

Mary (Wisniewski) Piechowski (Gertie's sister-in-law) — born 1910: That Wednesday afternoon, I was waiting for my daughter to get off the bus from school. I had left my five-year-old daughter, Albina, with a neighbor while I went to the bus stop. Meanwhile my daughter Florence, who was nine, had forgotten to get off the bus at her stop. She continued on down Thames Street a way. When she did get off the bus, the bartender at McGuiness's Bar saw her struggling in the wind and he took her in. We used to live near McGuiness', so the bartender knew Florence. He told her to stay there at the bar. It was too dangerous to be outside. Meanwhile, I had no idea where she was. When I returned home, I found that my neighbor had left my little daughter, Albina, all alone at my house. The neighbor had gone to take shelter with relatives elsewhere and had left my five-year-old daughter all by herself!

The New York, New Haven, and Hartford Railroad Station in Norwich. — *Dorothy Gravel*

Tom Piechowski (Mary's son) — born 1932: I was seven in 1938, and I remember walking home from kindergarten at the West Thames Street School, which was about a mile from our house on Commodore Street. As I started to walk up the hill on Perry Avenue, the wind was blowing so bad, that it blew me right back down the hill again! I tried another two or three times, but each time the wind just kept pushing me back down the hill. Finally, couple of high schoolers saw me, grabbed me by the arms, and pulled me up the hill so I could get home. That was one terrible storm.

Mary: Around the time I was waiting for my daughter to get off the bus, my husband, Walter, was coming home from work at the International Silver Company in Thamesville. The company had sent everyone home when the back wall of the factory blew down and part of the factory roof had been carried away in the wind along with the ventilators and chimneys. On his way home, the storm was so bad that Walter decided to take shelter in McGuiness' Bar. He was certainly surprised to find our daughter Florence there! Eventually, we were all reunited back home.

Due to the extreme damage to their building in Norwich, the International Silver Company told all of their employees from their factory in Norwich to report to one of their other factories. My husband was told to go to work in Florence, Massachusetts, for the next few months. He and several other men from Norwich would drive up together and spend the whole week working there. They would sleep at a boarding house during the week, and then on Friday they would drive home again. I was left to care for my three children alone from Monday to Friday. It was a stressful time, and it seemed kind of scary being alone. My brother, Joe, and his wife, Gertie, had been flooded out of their apartment on the East Side, so I asked them to come stay with us. They came with their two girls and stayed with me and my children, which worked out well for me. I didn't like being alone while my husband was away in Massachusetts. We gave Gertie and Joe's family our living room and dining room to use as their space, and they stayed with us through the winter.

Mary's parents, Dominica and Władysław Wisniewski, lived out in Preston on a farm on Prodell Road. On the following pages, her brothers, Ed, Walter, and Paul, and sisters, Martha and Helen, share their memories of the storm as well.

Ed Wisniewski — born 1922: Just a few weeks earlier, I had begun my second year of high school at NFA. When I returned home from school on that rainy Wednesday, my mother sent me to meet my younger sister and brother on their way home from the Palmer School, a one-room schoolhouse that was about a mile away on Old Jewett City Road in Preston. My mother told me to bring them an umbrella and raincoats since it was raining so hard. On my way, the wind and rain were so bad that I stopped to take shelter under the Wilson's barn on Old Jewett City Road. As I stood there, a big gust of wind came and blew the barn right off its foundation and backward into the field. I must have closed my eyes when the wind came, because the next thing I knew, rain was falling on my head. I looked up and saw the barn I had been standing under was gone! I continued on up the hill to the schoolhouse, but no one was there, so I walked to the next farm up the road. No one there had seen my brother or sister either. There were all kinds of trees down everywhere, so I decided I had better head back home. Once I got there, I discovered that Walter and Martha had already returned home on their own.

> I must have closed my eyes when the wind came, because the next thing I knew, rain was falling on my head. I looked up and saw the barn I had been standing under was gone!

That the afternoon the sun came out like it was summer—it was just beautiful. We thought the worst was over, but that was only the eye of the hurricane. Pretty soon the eye had passed us and the storm started whacking us again. When the storm had finally calmed down for good, we had a chance to look around our farm. You wouldn't believe all the damage that storm had done. We saw that our horse barn had been blown down along with one of our chicken coops. Another cow barn that had stood right behind our house was gone as well. Fortunately our house made it through the storm with just a few shingles blown off.

That day of the hurricane turned out to be my last day of school. There was a lot of work to be done around the farm, so I stayed home to help my father rebuild the horse barn. Throughout the fall I continued to help at home, and eventually I decided to get a job instead of returning to school.

Left to right: Martha, Helen, and Walter Wisniewski.
— *Martha Jancewicz*

Walter Wisniewski — born 1929: I was ten years old in 1938. Me and my sister, Martha, had to walk home from the Palmer School in the storm. We didn't know our mother had sent our older brother Ed to look for us on the road, so instead of coming home on the roads, we cut through the fields. Back home, the walls of our house were swaying like ocean waves. Everyone in the house was praying out loud, hoping the storm would spare us.

Martha (Wisniewski) Jancewicz — born 1926.
The following is an entry from her diary:
"There was a hurricane in Preston on September 21, 1938, Wednesday at 3 o'clock in the afternoon. It blew trees up by the roots. Our new barn went into pieces, our chicken coops were blown away along with a few of the chickens. Only the house, garage, corncrib, and an old shed were left standing. I had to come home from school in the terrible hurricane. Oh, I was wet and scared! The whole family was afraid the house would blow away, but only a few shingles came off the roof. Our neighbor had it terrible, everything blew away, even the top of the house, and only a shed was standing. The next morning it seemed like we were starting life all over again."

Boat in front of the
Auditorium Hotel.
— from "New England
Hurricane, Federal
Writer's Project" by
Hale, Cushman,
and Flint

Helen (Wisniewski) Wojtkiewicz — born 1924: I remember walking up Prodell Road that afternoon after being dropped off by the bus from the Norwich Free Academy. Everything was unusually quiet—no wind, no birds, nothing. Then, all of a sudden came the terrible wind and heavy rain. When I got home my mother told my father to go out and try to do something to secure the garage. It was so bad out that he didn't want to leave the house. My mother finally convinced him that he had to go, so he took some of my brothers and they put boards around to support the garage. Our hay barn blew down along with all the hay. The chicken coop came down as well. The chickens were everywhere, and later we had to go round them all up again.

The storm had come up around 3 o'clock, and my mother didn't have time to make supper. She tried to get us to eat some pies she had made earlier that day—pumpkin and apple—but everyone was too afraid to eat. We all hid in our bedrooms away from the windows. We had a big black dog at the time and throughout the storm he just hid under the table or a bed. The following week my brother Peter drove us to the seashore to Misquamicut State Beach in Westerly, Rhode Island. The damage here was so devastating and unbelievable that there was practically no beach left—and no cottages either.

Paul Wisniewski — born 1920:

Paul was living in Preston and worked in Norwich.

I was working at the Boston Bakery on the West Side of Norwich when the storm hit. I didn't get home until afternoon the next day. Thames Square was flooded ten feet deep. I had to go by rowboat from Thames Square to Washington Square, then across the Laurel Hill Bridge, to Talman Street, to the East Side, and up Hamilton Avenue. You couldn't go through downtown, at all because it was still flooded. There was a big coal barge in the street in the middle of the square. Once I made it through the flooded areas of the city, then I had to get through all the downed trees and wire. I was climbing over trees all the way home.

When I finally returned to the farm, I told the rest of my family how all the roads were flooded and there were trees down everywhere. That was the first time my family realized just how extensive the damage from the storm had been. Power was out everywhere down city. We didn't have power yet out on the farm in Preston, so at least that part didn't bother us.

> **Weeks later all the red cedar trees on the farm turned brown on one side from salt spray which had been blown in all the way from the ocean!**

Every building on our farm had been wrecked except the house. The house was a wreck, too, but it was still standing. We found some of our chickens in the pasture and out in the woods with half of their feathers torn off. The strangest thing was that weeks later all the red cedar trees on the farm turned brown on one side from salt spray that had been blown in all the way from the ocean—and our farm was at least twenty miles away from the coast!

The front of the
Finn Block in
Jewett City, Conn.
— the Griswold
Historical Society

BEYOND NORWICH

The devastation in Norwich is just part of the story. The 1938 Hurricane tore a huge path of destruction throughout New England. Below are stories from people who lived in communities outside of the city.

Griswold/Jewett City, Connecticut

Alice A. Brown — born 1878

Alice A. Brown was the secretary at Riverside Grammar School in Jewett City, Connecticut. The following is an excerpt from her diary submitted by Mary Rose Deveau, Alice Brown's great-niece. The notes in parenthesis and postscript were added by Mary Rose to clarify the story.

"**Wednesday, September 21:** Hurricane! Another day of rain. Very muggy. At 2 Linn was getting flood news from Hartford, Brockville, etc. (on the radio). High wind. She said we must be getting the tail end of the forecast tropical hurricane. At 3:15 it was so blowy, I sent one (school) bus along, but it didn't get through. As I was on the sheltered side of the school, I did not realize the force of the storm. Trees were already down in the schoolyard. Took in Mrs. Hiscox, Margaret, two Armstrongs, and Harold, (her grandnephew) and went to see high water at bridge. Tree down on Main Street, on bridge, and Miss Sharkey's shed. Branches falling all around us. Delivered my guests and had to squeeze between branches coming back from Culver's. Car rocked so it scared me. Ashland Lake covered with high waves and whitecaps. As I drove in the yard, I saw the ash tree down and began to weep. Linn rushed me out of the garage as the wind was forcing my maple tree against it so that it was going off the foundation. As we entered the house, the stained-glass window (over the piano) fell in. I covered the piano with a blanket. After that window was

covered and I had gathered up the books, pictures, and draperies, I sat on the couch with the children (Harold aged nine, Mary Rose aged five, and Bill aged two), while Linn and Sam rushed from cellar to attic, boarding up five more windows. As they finished the last one, the big maple tree finally uprooted without doing any more damage than breaking a little of the cornice of the house, smashing windows, and pushing the garage two feet forward and twisting it. Linn and Sam were all in and I dosed them with aromatic ammonia, which disturbed Harold more than the hurricane. He kept asking if it would last a week; it lasted about three hours, not counting the high wind earlier and until dark.

"Lights and telephone departed early and we went without for two weeks, using candles, lamps, and flashlights.

"We did not realize then how serious it was, but thought our exposed position made it worse for us. None of us could eat supper. Harold and Mary Rose were sleeping in the parlor, as their windows were smashed, boarded, and bits of fine glass all around.

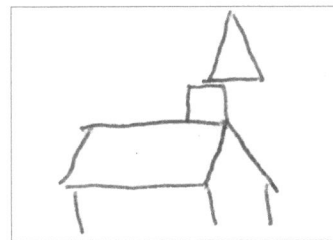

Above: Alice Brown's sketch of St. Mary's church.

Left: photo showing damage to St. Mary's steeple.
— *the Griswold Historical Society*

"Watched men cut away big tree across Brown Avenue so traffic could go that way. North Main Street shut off because St. Mary's spire looked like this. Besides the ash and maple, I lost my three tall spruces and my sweet pear tree.

"**Thursday, September 22:** What a sight! Could not get a (camera) film to take anything but my own backyard. Chopped the way to the back door through the tree. Priscilla's (Hodge) folks were here in Jewett City all night. Everybody was after Sam (he was a carpenter). He spent the morning on our roof and then fixed two more temporarily. I drove downtown—roundabout way—to see the awful sight. Everybody either sightseeing, on a ladder, or swinging an ax. Bucky (Lloyd Buckingham) up for Sam to go to Ross's. Says the Leonards (who were at their cottage at a Rhode Island beach) were washed out to sea. No papers.

"**Friday, September 3:** Mrs. Leonard is dead, Fred alive. Bond bread men chopped their way for ten miles to get to their truck. Stopped work long enough to look at textile (mill just down the road from her house). Priscilla helped me rake. I have an awful cold.

"**Saturday, September 24:** Lovely. Dragged branches out to the garden. Otis (Littlefield) came this p.m. and got the tree off the house. The trunk is straightening out and so was the garage. We had a lamp, a candle, and a flashlight on each floor."

Postscript by Mary Rose Deveau

And so it went. Work progressed slowly. Everything had to be done by hand. It was many months before all the damage around town was repaired. None of the churches replaced their tall steeples or belfries. The Second Congregational Church on Main Street was so badly damaged it had to be demolished.

Priscilla Goodenough

Excerpts from a letter by Priscilla Goodenough to her sister Virginia Fosberg, which was submitted by Pahl Rice. She describes her experience getting through the storm. The church mentioned is the Second Congregational Church in Griswold, Connecticut.

"Got home about 3 o'clock, just in time. For the next three hours, it was bedlam doubled. Trees bent. Rain swirled in sheets so that at times you couldn't see anything. The wind made the most awful roaring sound, so that even in the house—with the noise shut out— you had to yell to be heard.

"We saw trees crash one after another in Young's yard (about five I guess), branches crack and topple, electric signs go crashing to the street, all the cables drop and wires hang, swaying back and forth… The church got it quite a bit. First the cross at the top snapped

Left: the Second Congregational Church in Griswold, Conn.
— *Pahl Rice*

Below: demolition of the church.
— *the Griswold Historical Society*

off, then that big stained glass window was entirely blown in and one above the tower door. In the height of the storm, the tiles on the roof and steeple looked as if some mighty hand had ruffled them the wrong way.

"Luckily, Pa had his car out in front. The garage didn't go over, but it swayed plenty, and tile and bricks from the church rained on it."

Postscript

Inspection by architects determined that the cost of repairs to the church was prohibitive. The congregation could not raise the funds, and after serious consideration, it was voted to sell the land and the ruined building. The organ, bell, and furnishings were not sold to the developer who eventually built the building that currently houses the Jewett City Pharmacy and the State Theatre.

Philip Russi — born 1934

I was about four years old in the fall of 1938. My family lived in Jewett City on Palmer Avenue. The building we lived in had eight apartments in it and sits on top of a hill, which is one of the highest points in the city. My brother and I lived there with my parents, Euclid and Agnes, in a third-floor apartment. I can remember during the storm my family went down into the cellar of the building along with all the other people who lived in our whole apartment block.

> **All of the windows were broken, and the beds in our bedrooms were covered in seaweed and sand! Seaweed and sand—and our house was about thirty miles from the ocean.**

After the storm settled down, we went back upstairs to our apartment. All of the windows were broken, and the beds in our bedrooms were covered in seaweed and sand! Seaweed and sand—and our house was about thirty miles from the ocean. There was a lot of damage everywhere, trees blown over, and cars flipped on their sides. My mother was pregnant then. She had my younger brother just a week later on September 28, 1938.

Charles Butremovic — born 1923

I was about fifteen years old in 1938, and was at Griswold High School when it started raining. We got out of school about 3 o'clock. We didn't have any bus transportation then. I was living over on the other side of Jewett City, on Russell Street, which was a good mile and a half from school. As me and a couple of the guys who lived in my neighborhood started walking

home, it started raining a little harder. We got as far as what was called Finn's Block, and we thought we'd wait there a little bit to see if the rain would let up—but it didn't. Then once the wind started picking up real hard, we decided we better get out of there. We left Finn's Block, and started running home. Trees were coming down, and there were shingles flying all over the place.

We finally got home. The house I lived in had a double porch that ran the whole length of the house. There came a good gust of wind and it blew the top porch roof off and threw it over the top of the house. It landed way up in the back field. Some of the pieces of the roof ended up about a quarter of a mile away. There had been big corner poles on that porch and we later found them hundreds and hundreds of yards off in the fields.

There was a man who had a plot of land across from our garden. He had a shed there where he kept all his equipment. I happened to be in the doorway in the back of our house looking out over the yard, when the wind lifted that whole shed up and blew it right across the road. It

The corner of Green Avenue and Mechanic Street in Jewett City, Conn. The cars belonged to Harris Palmer, a teacher at Griswold High School.
— the Griswold Historical Society

hit a telephone pole and was smashed into little pieces. That whole building went right up into the air in one piece. I tell you, there weren't many buildings that weren't hit somehow by that storm.

We had a family living upstairs, and the woman was up there with her two youngsters and a baby while her husband was at work. They came down the stairs and started running across the backyard where we had our garden, way out in the back. I ran off after them and when I caught up to her, I took the baby from her arms, and ran with them. We had to go through some water that was up to our knees in some places. We ran for cover to a house that was back there, and we stayed there until the hurricane died down. Why it was me that ran out there with that baby, I don't know.

The damage that storm done! There used to be a big Protestant church on Main Street in Jewett City. It was just as big as St. Mary's, and it had a big steeple up in the air. That church had so much damage in the storm that they had to demolish it. St. Mary's church used to have a big tall steeple, too. That was also damaged in the hurricane, and they ended up cutting it down to what it is today. Our movie theater had been in Finn's Block. That had so much damage that they had to close it up. For a while, they showed movies at the high school instead.

After the storm died down, us neighborhood boys went out to see some of the damage. We took a walk down to the Aspinook Mill. There was a big dam there, and the river was so high that the water was almost even on both sides of the dam. It was flowing straight across the top.

Back then, people didn't call them hurricanes. They called them line storms. These were storms that the changing of the seasons brought on—from summer to fall or winter to spring.

Preston, Connecticut

Winthrop Benjamin — born 1929

I was almost ten years old at the time of the hurricane, and I attended the Brown School, a one-room schoolhouse over by the Preston Trading Post. The Brown School was the lower grades—grades one through four. Grades five through eight were at the Preston City School house, which is where my sisters Jennie and Hester went. I recall sitting in class with our music teacher, Miss Barnes, as we were looking out the window watching the tops of the trees swaying to and fro.

I do remember that was a rough week. It rained for about three days—on and off, on and off, on and off... I guess that was the coming of the big storm. Back then, people didn't call them hurricanes. They called them line storms. These were storms that the changing of the seasons brought on—from summer to fall, or from winter to spring. Some of them line storms could be quite severe.

My mother, Minnie, was down in Westerly, Rhode Island, visiting my sister Carrie, who was in training there to become a registered nurse at the Westerly Hospital. There was a bus called the Tally Ho Line that used to travel from Norwich to Westerly. My mother had a round-trip ticket, and the bus driver said to her, "If you didn't have a round-trip ticket, I wouldn't leave Westerly. I'd stay right here, because I probably won't get home." And he was right. I believe he had to sleep in his bus that night. They got as far as Route 164 and Route 2, and then the bus driver stopped the bus and said to her, "This is it. This is as far as I'm going."

As she was walking home, an acquaintance saw her, picked her up, and drove her as far as Fred Blue's house. The Blues were good friends of ours. It was getting to be about 4 o'clock, so she figured she better stay there for the night. Of course, she was wondering how us children were doing, but the good Lord took care of us. There were two giant maple trees in our front yard. They could've fallen right on the house and us kids could have been in some trouble, but the good Lord does nice things. He dumped those trees over, but he did not put them on the house. He laid them right alongside the front of the house, and that's a miracle. Next morning, first shot, our mother walked home. When she got there, she started to cry. Two portions of our roof had come off the house and ended up way across the road in the trees, yet the house was still sound, and we were all safe inside.

My brother Jared did carpentry work, and about six months before that hurricane ventured in, he had built Ray Krug two beautiful chicken coops. Lord knows, that storm picked those chicken coops up with all the chickens inside of them. It carried them across his property, and they ended up in the trees behind his house. Only a 120 mile an hour wind could do that, and that's what we had during that storm. Unfortunately, the hurricane laid a lot of expenses on Ray's shoulders. It was sorrowful, but he bounced back. After that, he put big cables over those chicken coops to keep them down.

George Fritz had a farm on a dirt road off of Krug Road. He had a barn that was pretty feeble. It was old, old and was about to tumble down anyway. He had Arthur Parks, a great barn builder, build him a new barn. It wasn't a great huge one, but a beautiful one. Now, you're not going to believe this, but it's the truth. Just that day, they had moved the cows from his old barn into the new one. They moved everything—the grain and the whole nine yards—when low and behold, here comes the '38 Hurricane. It flattened that poor new barn to bits.

> Lord knows that storm picked those chicken coops up with all the chickens inside of them and carried them across his property. They ended up in the trees behind his house. Only a 120 mile an hour wind could ever do that. After that he put big cables over those chicken coops to keep them down.

The storm did a lot of damage to our church, the Preston City Congregational Church. There were big horse sheds beside the building. People back then would drive their horse and buggies—*clippity-clop, clippity-clop*—to church and they would park them in those sheds. Parts of those sheds got destroyed in the storm. Later, my brother and Mike Pannis set up a new side on the shed. The church lost probably four or five stalls, but at least we still had some horse stalls to use for cold rainy days.

My aunt and uncle, Herbert and Florence Benjamin, used to own some little cottages over on Amos Lake that they rented out in the summer. They had little rowboats they would rent out, too, for fifty cents a boat. That was their income. Well, the 1938 Hurricane blew all those cottages away—good-bye Charlie!

The eye of the storm was beautiful—clear, sunshine, just beautiful sunshine, But then in about a half hour, the storm came back. You know, the tail of that storm was just as severe as the front. We were outside, and we had to get back in the house right quick. You have to look out for the tail of a storm like that. It will give you a kick.

Years ago farmers used to annex buildings onto their house, so in the bad weather—in the sleet and the rain—they wouldn't have to walk outside to their barn to do their chores. Our house was like that. We had a carriage shed attached to our house. There was an undertaker in Norwich who used to rent space in our shed from my father so they could their park their hearse there. Whenever they had a funeral, they would put the casket on the back of a buggy and bring it out to our farm. They would load it in the hearse and then drive it back into town with their horses. It was a beautiful old hearse, and it is fortunate it wasn't in our shed during the hurricane, because that shed went right down. Our icehouse went down, too. My father used to cut ice over on Amos Lake in the wintertime. He would store the ice in the icehouse, and it would last all through the summer. Across the road from our house we had a fair-sized barn. My sister and I looked out at it once during the hurricane. Then when we looked out again a few minutes later, that barn was gone. It blew over into the woods. That storm raised a lot of havoc.

Most of the roads in Preston were cleared in about a week or so. That was because most people weren't bashful to say, "I have a saw. I can come and help." Everybody chipped in because they knew darn well if they didn't help, it wouldn't be just one week that the roads would be closed, it would be more like two weeks. So it was to everyone's benefit to come out and help clear the trees. I know my brothers helped out, and a good many others did, too. If a barn went down and someone didn't have a place to put their cattle, they would drive them down the road to someone else's barn, so that they could milk them or grain them. They were nice people years ago, and everybody tried to help each other out. God bless them, to see how they all worked together to pull us out of this mess. It was a great, great thing.

Bill Muttart — born 1934

Bennett's Store in the center of Preston. — *from the collection of Faith Jennings*

You might think that me being only four years old when that storm hit that I wouldn't remember much, but I do! I was staying with my grandparents Sterry and Belle Pierce at their farm on Pierce Road in Preston, Connecticut. My other grandfather was Rev. William L. Muttart, the pastor of the Congregational Church in Preston. I would stay with my grandparents on their farm for a few days at a time, and I happened to be with them on that day. Around mid-day, somehow my Grandmother Belle had heard that there was a hurricane coming. She told me to run out to the outhouse and tell my grandpa that a hurricane was coming. I had never heard that word before, and based on how she was acting, I went out and told him what I thought she had said: "Grandpa, a hurry cane is coming!"

Several hours later I was sitting with my grandparents in their living room watching the storm out the window. We kept seeing bricks flying through the air and wondered where those bricks could be coming from. Grandma and I went up to the second floor of their house, and when she opened the door to the attic, there was nothing but storm clouds above us! The whole roof and the chimney were gone!

Shortly after, two men who lived nearby came up to my grandparent's farm to help us. They escorted my grandparents to their car. One of them took me and held me under his arm while he crawled on his hands and knees, steadying himself against the wind with his hand on the foundation of the house or clutching the sod. We all drove over to Bennett's Store, which was about two miles away, in the center of Preston City. There were trees falling on the road, but we managed to get around them. At the store, we found a number of people had gathered there, including the store owner, Earl Bennett, and my mother, Edith. My parents had bought a home on North Stonington Road in Preston a just few months earlier in June. My mother had been home alone that day, so she decided to go take cover at Bennett's Store. We all went down to the dark basement of the store where we spent the night, using a candle for light, while waiting for the storm to subside.

Back on my grandparent's farm, the cow barn was completely blown down and the horse barn had been picked up and blown off its foundation. Considering all the damage done during that storm, nothing has quite approached it since.

Ledyard, Connecticut

Harold Crouch — born 1928

We were used to big storms coming through every year. My father referred to those storms as line storms, never hurricanes. That was the most unforgettable day for me. I was ten years old and was in class at the Ledyard Center Grammar School, a one-room schoolhouse by Town Hall. I had the same teacher for seven years, Evelyn Brisofski-Izbicki, who was from Norwich. That day started out very calm. The teacher did not dismiss us early, so we stayed in school. Pretty soon the trees started falling everywhere—across the highway and taking down the power lines with them. Towards the middle of the day, the winds got to be so strong that we couldn't even stand up.

My mother, Anna, was at home with my sister-in-law, who was pregnant at the time. They were sitting in an old car, and as they sat there, they saw our garage collapse right in front of them. The garage just fell over. After the storm passed, we had to right it and reconstruct the roof. My father, Herbert, had been away at work. He was self-employed as a stonemason, bricklayer, and plasterer. He also did cobblestone work. He laid much of the cobblestone you see in Mystic and Groton today. My father was a very busy man with all the repair work after that storm.

I remember looking out in the middle of the storm when the wind was really blowing hard and seeing my neighbor up on his roof nailing his roof down. He was afraid that roof was going to blow off.

All the trees were all stripped of their leaves from the powerful wind. We were just starting autumn when the storm hit, and that year there was no color in the trees at all.

We didn't lose power in our house, because before the storm, my brother had installed a DC, direct current, generator. We had our own well, so we had water after the storm, too. So unlike most people, we had all our facilities functioning in our home. I guess we had it pretty good after the hurricane. We could just sit back and watch all the destruction around us, while we had all the advantages that most people in the city didn't have.

One of the things I remember most is that all the trees were all stripped of their leaves from that powerful wind. We were just starting autumn when the storm hit, and that year there was no color in the trees at all.

Gales Ferry, Groton, and New London, Connecticut

Richard Pfannenstiel — born 1924
(see page 119)

I had just started my first year of high school at NFA. I remember it was pouring rain outside, so I was waiting in Slater Hall for my bus to come. There had been a great big elm tree in front of the school near the sidewalk where the buses used to come in. It was right in front of the Main building. We called it the "cigarette tree," because that's where all the guys used to go and smoke. I saw my bus pull in, and, as I was running out to it, that massive elm went down—just before I got to the bus. That was my first memory that something really bad was happening. We all got on the bus quick, and as we were driving home I remember all the trees and branches coming down on the road. Some of the windows on the bus blew out. I lived on Route 12 in Allyn's Point over in Gales Ferry. Somehow we managed to make it home alright.

My father, Alois, was a bookkeeper at Shetuket Lumber, up on North Main Street. He was there with the other men working away when suddenly the roof blew off the building. I guess that meant it was time for him to go home. He got in his car and made it as far as Laurel Hill. He couldn't drive any further because of all the trees across the road. He had to walk home from there—over trees and under trees. He had a terrible time crossing the drawbridge, because there were waves breaking right over the bridge. The water there was tremendous. When he finally got home, it was just getting dark. I remember he walked all around the outside of our house to make sure everything was OK, and it was. Our house didn't have any damage. Then he walked

over to the Pringles, our neighbors across the street. Half of their barn was blown away, and the other half was in the street. The roof was off Waterman's barn, too.

My aunt Belle, Belle Riley, lived with us. She was at a meeting over on Star Hill in Groton. Star Hill was across from the river and on a hill—up way high. The wind was blowing really strong up there. From up on top of the hill, she could look across the river at New London, which was on fire at the time. It was a terrible fire. The wind was blowing over a hundred miles an hour. The firemen didn't have a chance. The odd thing about a hurricane is that when the eye of the storm passed, the winds turned around and blew in the opposite direction, pushing the fire back into the area it had already burned. They were lucky that happened. If the winds hadn't changed directions, half of New London would have burnt to the ground.

Aunt Belle and the other ladies had to walk home from Groton, because all the roads were closed. They walked up Route 12, as far as the sub base. They went right through the sub base, which was how the road went then. When they got up to Long Cove, the bridges were

Trees down in front of Slater at NFA.
— *NFA Mirror, 1940*

Wind, Fire, Water Ruin New London

(Special to The Bulletin)

New London, Sept. 22—Fire, death and destruction in monstrous proportions, riding with the first hurricane ever to have struck New England, laid waste to this city and vicinity doing damage estimated at between four and five millions of dollars here and perhaps doubling it in the surrounding area.

So stupendous was the whole thing that people were to-day gazing uncomprehendingly at a city that many of them had known for more than a half century. Trees that had sheltered its homes since the days of the Revolutionary war, and before, laid stark upon their sides showing their tremendous roots for the first time. School houses were terribly damaged, home interiors were drenched, a whole roof was a rare sight for miles around.

FIRE SWEEPS BANK STREET

As if the terrific ravages of the hurricane itself were not enough to satisfy the fates, the torn and twisted city sizzled under a roaring flame of fire, which destroyed building after building, shed after shed, and every other burnable object along the east side of Bank sreet, from the New London Grain Co. nearly to the Aben Hardware store.

It was without doubt New London's fiercest fire since Arnold burned the town. Tall, terrible, roaring flames, driven on by the hurricane made Bank street and the waterfront a thing of stark terror, as the city was placed under martial

Left: New London with Bank Street on fire in the midst of the hurricane. Over a quarter square mile of the city burned.
— *photograph from "The 1938 Hurricane an Historical and Pictorial Summary" by William Elliott Minsinger M.D.*

Above: article on the New London fire from the *Norwich Bulletin,* September 23, 1938.
— *from the collection of Norma Guile Kornacki*

$1,000,000 Fire Sweeps Bank Street District

excerpt of article from New London Day, September 22, 1938

The loss occasioned by the conflagration that raged during the afternoon and night resulted in damage estimated by officials of the fire department as "well in excess of $1,000,000." It broke out at 4:30 p.m. and was still smoldering this afternoon although it was brought under control shortly after midnight.

It laid waste practically the entire east side of Bank Street from the Armstrong or old Orpheum Theater building to the yard of the Central Coal Co., leaped across Bank Street and sent sparks that ignited structures in Tulley, Starr, and Green Streets and threatened the entire business area with destruction.

The origin of the fire is not definitely known although it is believed to have its start either in the Humphrey and Cornell building in Sparyard Street, the Sisk building, or in one of the coal pockets of the F. H. & A. Chappell Coal Co. At any rate, it appears as though these two buildings and the entire Chappell Coal and Lumber yard burst into flames simultaneously and within a few minutes the fire had developed into a holocaust.

The lumber, coal yard, the office buildings in front, the Sisk, and Humphrey and Cornell buildings were quickly destroyed completely. Next in the path of the flames was the station of the Niagara Engine Co. and the building of the Putum Furniture Co. and the flames, fanned into a white heat by the terrible wind, quickly destroyed both of these structures.

The fire then mushroomed out in all directions and gutted the building at 308 Bank Street, occupied by the New London Grain Co. This building adjoins that of the Putum concern.

Sparks ignited the roof of Thompson's garage across Bank Street from the Niagara Engine Co. and the building quickly went up in flames together with a number of automobiles stored therein. The fire ranging through the Chappell yard, communicated to the four story brick building occupied by the Plaut-Cadden Furniture Co. and the woodworking establishment of Nasetta Bros. in the rear of the furniture company's building.

The Nasetta building was razed and all that remained of the furniture concern's building and its vast stock of merchandise was the four bare walls and the debris littered floors.

The building occupied by the Eaton & Wilson Co. was also completely gutted as was the next building occupied by the Cheney-Packer fish market, the State Lunch, and another store. The flames then swept backwards to consume the coal pockets of the Central Coal Co.

The large alleyway separating the office of the coal company from the State Lunch, served as a stop gap for the flames, but sparks flew northwards and set fire in the roof of Aben Hardware building at 116 Bank Street occupied by the Bruce Electric Co. The situation at this point was so threatening that the fire department officials prepared to use dynamite in knocking down several buildings that were in danger, but the wind suddenly shifted…

Above: Humphrey and Cornell wholesale grocers in New London, Conn. One of the first buildings that burned in the fire.

Left: damaged buildings in New London.

— *both photographs by Richard Woodworth*

Tree down on a car in Griswold, Conn.
— *the Griswold Historical Society*

washed out, so they had to take the old dirt road back through the woods. There were all kinds of trees and bushes they had to walk around and over. My aunt and the other ladies were pretty old—probably in their sixties. She had a terrible time getting home. It was pitch black when she finally made it back. Her clothes were all ripped and torn, and she was exhausted. I remember that all she wanted to do was to sit down and have a cup of tea.

All the power lines were down, and everything was totally destroyed outside. My mother was all concerned. She wanted to know what we were going to do. My father said, "We're not going to do anything now. There's nothing we *can* do. We're just going to go to bed, wake up tomorrow, and then we'll see what we can do." So that's what we did. We went to bed. When we got up the next morning, it was like that line from the Wizard of Oz, when Dorothy says, "I don't think we're in Kansas anymore." That's what it looked like in Allyn's Point. All the trees were down. There were barns blown over. All the power lines were down. It was like a war zone. All those great big trees we used to have were down. My father and I cut up a lot of them trying to clear part of Route 12. We were just using handsaws. It must have taken four or five days before Route 12 was opened to traffic again. Everyone was a farmer back then, and everyone cut wood, so they knew how to deal with it. Across the street was a man who had a sawmill, and they were experts at cutting trees. They cut them into big pieces and left them along the side of

the road so cars could get through. Then they came back to finish the job later in the fall. Many people burned wood back then, so those big piles on the side of the roads all slowly disappeared over the years. One of the reasons we lost so many trees during the storm was that they still had all their leaves on them. There was a lot of wind resistance, and that made them fall over easier. Geeze, it was something!

I remember exactly a week after the storm I was sitting with my family having dinner by candlelight—when suddenly we heard the refrigerator click on. We had been surviving OK, but it sure was good to have the power back on.

Street Scene in New London, Conn. — *photograpgh by Richard Woodworth*

Canterbury, Connecticut

Eleanor (Havel) Mikutel — born 1932

On the day of the hurricane, I was at the Westminster Hill School in Canterbury, Connecticut. Westminster Hill was a one-room schoolhouse with eight grades and one teacher. The teacher had let us out early, because it was raining so hard. As my sister, Allie, and I were walking home, we saw my father, George, on the road. He was coming to find us. He called out: "What's the matter with the two of you?! Why are you out walking? Don't you know this is a bad storm!" What did I know? I was just six years old.

Our father took us home and had our whole family get into the car. He thought that was safer than being in the house. He had us bring pillows out there to put against the car windows to protect us in case anything hit them. As we all sat there together in the car, I remember looking at the large chicken coop we had in our yard, and seeing the coop lift up and fly into the air upside down. We had a cow that was staked out in the yard. My father kept looking at which way the cow was facing, and he would point the car in that same direction. I guess cows know to face into the wind, and my father, who had been a sailor, may have gotten the idea from sailing. He didn't want us to get broadsided. That cow told us which direction to go!

Bozrah, Connecticut

Jean (Kuchy) Len — born 1930

My family lived in Bozrah on Bishop Road. Our house was on a hillside with woods behind us. I remember we could hear the wind coming through the trees even before we knew there was going to be a storm. We could hear the wind in the leaves and then started to hear the trees falling. For several days before the storm, we had very wet weather which had made the ground around the roots of the trees very soft. That made all those trees blow over very easily when that wind started to blow.

He dug a little more into the hay pile and it was filled with snakes! They must have gone into the hay to take shelter during the hurricane.

We had cattle on our farm, and a few days before the storm, my father, Michael, had cut the hay. He had filled our barn until there was no more room, and then he juat piled the rest of the hay out in the yard. Surprisingly, that hay didn't blow away in the storm, I guess because it was such a large pile. After things quieted down, my father went and dug into the pile of hay and a snake came out. He dug in another spot and another snake came out. He dug a little more into the hay pile and it was filled with snakes! They must have gone into the hay to take shelter during the hurricane. That was quite strange. My father wasn't afraid of killing snakes, but when they all started coming out, I think it was even too much for him!

Franklin, Connecticut

Clara Hopkins — born 1928

I was ten years old when the hurricane hit, and my family lived in Franklin, Connecticut, at the time. I remember it had rained a lot for a few days before the storm. The roads weren't paved then, and after all that rain, there were big gullies on the sides of all the dirt roads. We lived just a few houses up from the Pautipaug School, which was the school I went to. There was a big pine tree that got knocked down in the storm, and it fell right on my school. After that we had to be bused to another school up on Route 32, towards Willimantic.

My father worked in the Baltic mills. The bridge to get to the mill was washed out in the storm. The people who lived on the other side had to set up a pulley so they could get supplies across the river. Since that bridge was gone, my father didn't return to work right away, because he would have had to go quite a way, probably down to Occum, just to cross the river.

North Grosvenor Dale, Connecticut

Norm Babbitt — born 1929

I was in the fourth grade then, and most of us students walked home from school. By 3:30 that afternoon, the wind was really zipping. I went to the house of my friend, Paul Hoar, who lived next door to me. His mother said I had better go home because of the storm. My house was only about a thousand feet away from there, but I really had to lean into the wind to make it home.

My family lived at 54 Holmes Street in North Grosvenor Dale, Connecticut. That was part of what was called Swede Village, an area of town owned by the Grosvenor Dale Company textile mill. About eighty percent of the houses were rented by Swedes who worked at the mill. The employees paid thirty-five cents a week out of their paychecks to the mill company for rent.

Due to the heavy rains, the water from French River started backing up into Back Water Brook, making it almost like a small lake. The wind was so strong that it was picking up water from the brook and slamming it against the second-floor windows of our house—which was about two thousand feet from the brook. We had to put blankets up against the windows, because the windows were actually bending! We saw the steeple from the Methodist Church of

Damage to a church in Mystic, Conn.
— *photograph by Richard Woodworth*

North Grosvenor Dale fly past our house and go into the brook. The steeple from the Lutheran Church on Main Street was also ripped off. It fell right between two houses.

During the storm, my father, Albert, along with Cliff Svenning and Zachy Alim were over at the cemetery burying a relative of ours, a woman named Doga Freudenthal. They had dug the grave and lowered the casket into the hole. The storm got too strong for them to be out in the open, so they all had to leave the cemetery in a hurry. They left the grave open, and it wasn't until a week later that they were able to go back to fill her grave in properly.

The next morning we saw all of the destruction in the area. A couple of hundred acres of yellow pines were all pulled up out of the ground. On our street, four oak trees fell into the road. Fortunately, they didn't hit any houses, but they looked like a bird's nest the way they piled up on each other. When we went downtown, we saw all the flooding. The north end of my school, the Thompson Public School, had been torn completely off. I remember you could look right inside and see the desks sitting there. We didn't have school for a month after. When we did finally go back to school, I was sent to St. Joseph's School for the rest of the year. The fifth graders went to another school, and the sixth graders went to a different school. Our school wasn't repaired until the following year.

In early 1939, a large sawmill was set up behind Swede Village. Many Canadian men came down to work there for twenty cents an hour. They came to make lumber out of all the acres of large pine trees that had been felled by the hurricane.

Sturbridge, Massachusetts

Mary (Suprenant) Abdellah — born 1929

We lived in Sturbridge, Massachusetts, on Podunk Road. My mother, Ruth, was eight months pregnant and already had seven of us children at home: George, Doris, Donald, me, Lucy, Gerald, and Sylvia. She had been home making apple pies and the chimney caught on fire. Our neighbors, the Augers, had two turkeys, and I remember that it was raining so hard that those turkeys wanted to come right inside of our house! That night my father was afraid to let us sleep upstairs, so he took some blankets and had the three of us girls sleep on the piano while my brothers slept on the floor.

I remember the day after the storm was beautiful! My father, George, and several neighbors spent the next several days cutting away all the maple trees that had fallen in the road. It took them three days just to clear three miles. In our yard, we lost five fruit trees: three apple and two pear, and our outhouse flew away in the storm. My father had to build a new one next to the garage in the back. A while later, we had a new chimney built. My new little brother, Oliver, was born just two weeks after that storm.

Providence, Rhode Island

Ina (Place) Macko — born 1924

I grew up in Providence, Rhode Island, and in 1938 I was fourteen years old and attended the Classical High School. After school that day, around 3 o'clock in the afternoon, I met my mother, Ina, and we went to the old Albee Theater in the center of Providence. Back then movies cost

Flooding around City Hall in downtown Providence, Rhode Island. — *photograph from "The Hurricane and Flood of September 21, 1938 at Providence, R.I." by Adler Art Associates*

fifteen cents. I always liked going to the Albee, because on the back of each of the seats there was a candy dispenser. You could put a nickel in and out the bottom would come those chocolate candies with the white dots on them—nonpareils.

My mother and I were sitting upstairs in the balcony watching the movie when all of a sudden the lights went out. When we looked down, we saw water pouring into the theater! All the people who had been sitting downstairs either ran out of the building or ran upstairs into the balcony with us. We knew we couldn't leave—we would have had to swim out—and my mother didn't know how to swim, so we just sat there and waited.

The Albee was an old-fashioned building, and on the walls there were gas jets from back in the days when they used gas lights. My mother was a worrier, and she worried that we would be gassed out. I tried to tell her that the gas jets weren't used anymore, but she was afraid that somehow the gas would start flowing.

It was scary being in the dark theater with the water rushing below us, but we had no idea why the water was coming in. We had no idea it was a hurricane. We probably would've been more scared if we had known.

We waited there until about 5 o'clock. By then, the water had receded and we were able to get out of the building. It was then that we saw that the whole city had really got doused in the storm. My uncle lived closer to the theater than we did, so we walked to his house and he took us home. When we went into our house it was dark; there were no lights. We looked around and found my father, Cyril, sleeping. My mother started yelling at him, "How could you sleep when your wife and daughter were out in this storm?!" My father said, "There were no lights. What could I do? I thought I would just go to sleep." My mother was so upset with him for that.

We had a family farm in Greene, Rhode Island, about a mile from the Connecticut border. My father's cousin

The Biltmore Hotel in downtown Providence, Rhode Island. — *photograph from "The Hurricane and Flood of September 21, 1938 at Providence, R.I." by Adler Art Associates*

took care of it for us. When the storm came, he opened the front and back doors to the barn and the garage so the wind could blow right through them during the storm. That trick must have worked, because many other barns were damaged, yet our barn and garage were still standing when the storm was over.

Cottages at Lord's Point in Stonington, Conn.
— *photographs by Richard Woodworth*

ALONG THE SHORE

The coastal areas of New England were especially hard hit by the Hurricane of 1938. They were first battered by the hurricane and then a tidal surge came and wiped out entire communities. Several coastal areas that had been densely packed with beach cottages and summer businesses before the storm were so badly damaged that they were never rebuilt. This happened in the oceanside communities of Watch Hill, Rhode Island, and Ocean Beach in New London, Connecticut. The land was taken over by the cities or states and turned into public beaches.

Lord's Point, Stonington, Connecticut

Kelvin and Rod Stott
(see page 43)

(see page 43)

Kelvin Stott, born 1936, and his brother Rod Stott, born 1939, tell what happened to their grandparents' cottage down at the shore at Lord's Point in Stonington, Connecticut.

Kelvin: My mother's parents, Frank and Annie Wheeler, lived on Scotland Road in Norwich, and they also had a cottage at Lord's Point. Their cottage, named "Annie" after my grandmother, was right on the shore. It had a little stone seawall in front of it, and behind it was a small road. Beyond the road ran the railroad tracks. Grandma and Grandpa were down at the cottage when the storm hit, and they had no warning that a hurricane was coming. When it started to get windy and blowy, Grandpa Wheeler said, "It's getting kind of nasty. We better get out of here." But Grandma Wheeler told him, "I can't go out there, I forgot my rubbers." So they stayed put. Pretty soon the water started coming up. It came up over the stone breakwater. It came up around the bottom of the house, and then it came up to around the bottom of the first-floor windows. The two of them thought, maybe the first floor was not a good place to be, so they went upstairs. The wind was blowing, and the water kept coming up some more. Pretty soon the water came up so high that the cottage started to float. As it was floating, the house turned about forty-five degrees so a corner of the house was facing the waves, like the bow of the boat. The waves were breaking on the bow of the house.

Rod: As the cottage was lifted up by the water, everything inside the house shifted. Grandma and Grandpa were upstairs in one of the bedrooms by then. They had a bureau upstairs that went zinging across the room as the house shifted. As it flew by, it broke the door knob off the door of the room they are in. So now they're upstairs in the bedroom of a house that is floating on the water, and they can't even open the door to the room!

> So now they're upstairs in the bedroom of a house that is floating on the water, and they can't even open the door to the room!

When the storm was over, the cottage ended up back on shore, on the embankment for the railroad tracks, just behind where the cottage had stood. Grandpa stepped out onto the roof of the back porch. He climbed down and somehow found a ladder and helped grandma down on to the railroad tracks. Mind you, grandma and grandpa weren't young. They were probably in their seventies at that time. After the storm, they had the house dragged back onto its foundation just as it had been.

Kelvin: There were about six or seven other houses right near them in a row. After the storm none of them were there anymore. Those houses had been washed out to Long Island Sound either whole or in pieces. I think Grandma and Grandpa may have been the only ones down there during the storm. The only ones foolish enough to stay. Many of the cottages at Lord's Point were just used as summer residences. Since it was already towards the end of September, all the other people may have gone back to their homes already.

Opposite: the Wheeler's cottage "Annie" at Lord's Point. This photo was taken about 1940, after it drifted away in the 1938 hurricane and was put back.

Back row, left to right: Grandpa Frank Wheeler with hat and tie, Robert Stott Jr., and Grandma Annie Wheeler.

Front row: Shirley Santo, Kelvin Stott, Evelyn Stott Santo, Grace Stott, and Natalie Santo holding the baby, Rod Stott.
— *Kelvin Stott*

115

Opposite and above: Groton Long Point, Groton, Conn.
— *photographs by Edward & Mary Carlson*

Left: the tracks of the New Haven Railroad along the shore in Niantic, Conn.
— *from "A Photographic Record of the New England Hurricane and Flood, New England's Greatest Disaster" by The Conn. Circle Magazine*

Right: cottage flipped onto its side at Ocean Beach, New London, Conn.
— *photograph by Richard Woodworth*

Opposite: view of Ocean Beach.
— *photograph by Edward & Mary Carlson*

Article on Ocean Beach from the *Norwich Bulletin*, September 23, 1938.
— *from the collection of Norma Guile Kornacki*

Ocean Beach, New London, Connecticut

Richard Pfannenstiel — born 1924
(see page 98)

A little while after the storm, we had heard how hard Ocean Beach had been hit, so my father decided to take us down and have a look. Ocean Beach originally used to be a real big honky-tonk. There was a merry-go-round and little places that sold seafood or ice cream. There were bar rooms and dance halls where all the big orchestras used to play—all kinds of things. And of course, it was a great beach for swimming. Us kids used to have a real good time down there.

After the hurricane, we saw everything that had been on Ocean Beach was now piled up high, way back where the parking lot is today. The boardwalk was gone. Even the road going into that area was gone. Nothing survived at all. New London didn't know what to do with it. Eventually the city took over the property and decided to turn it into the beach that we have today.

Ocean Beach Wiped Out

Perhaps the worst sight to behold from a standpoint of sheer destruction was Ocean Beach, a fortnight ago, a resort, teeming with thousands, today a shambles. Its cottages were no more than a twisted, torn, pulverized mass of wood and metal and glass, and the entire section was under water from the terrible advance of the ocean.

Scenes from Ocean
Beach, New London,
Conn.

— *photograph on
opposite top by
Raymond R. Carlson*

— *photographs on
opposite bottom and
this page by Edward &
Mary Carlson*

Watch Hill and Misquamicut, Rhode Island

Irene (Duhaime) Radzvilowicz — born 1928
(see page 3)

A few weeks after the storm, my family took a ride down by Atlantic Beach and Misquamicut. All those little houses that had been there were washed out in the storm. There had been a church there, St. Clare's Chapel on Crandell Avenue, and I had heard that all the people from the cottages went into the church during the hurricane. They thought the church was stronger than their little cottages on the beach, so they all congregated there. That church washed away, too. Quite a few people lost their lives there.

My family used to go to Atlantic Beach often before the storm. All our relatives would meet at the beach. The women and kids would stay on the beach while the men, my father and uncles, would go over to the cove and be scrunging [sic] for clams—digging for them with their feet. I never could do that! Misquamicut just wasn't the same after that hurricane. All those nice houses that were there were just gone…

Opposite: St Clare's Chapel before and after the storm.
— *from "The Hurricane, September 21, 1938, Westerly, Rhode Island and Vicinity, Historical and Pictorial" by Lewis R. Greene*

Below: cottage at Misquamicut.
— *photograph by Edward & Mary Carlson*

WATCH HILL

A broad expanse of sand where once stood 44 beautiful homes on Napatree Point told the major story of the ordeal of wind and water which struck Watch Hill, causing fifteen residents to lose their lives.

Swept clean and bare even of foundations by the mountainous seas which carried cottages and buildings across Little Narragansett Bay, the Fort Road, one of the most exclusive streets of this resort, presented a grim panorama the morning after the storm.

The series of waves, each higher than the previous one, were lashed into a seething, foaming fury to a height of 30 feet. An observer saw all the cottages on Napatree Point topple before this sea within a period of 15 minutes. The waters of the bay backed over the sea wall, flooded Bay Street to a depth of three feet and only a shattered heap of lumber and broken blocks of concrete were left on the bathing beach. The Watch Hill Beach Club and the Watch Hill Yacht Club, handsomest of the resort buildings, were victims, and pleasure yachts were tossed helter skelter on Bay Street. Cottages around the Lighthouse Point were undermined and on East Beach three more were demolished by the driving waves.

The summary of loss of cottages illustrates where the disaster hit hardest—Fort Road, 44; Larkin Road, 3; Manatuck Avenue, 3, and Off Ocean View Highway, 3. A total of 53.

Opposite: Watch Hill, Rhode Island, before and after the storm.

Left: article on Watch Hill.

— *all from "The Hurricane, September 21, 1938, Westerly, Rhode Island and Vicinity, Historical and Pictorial" by Lewis R. Greene*

Below: damage at Watch Hill.
— *photograph by Edward & Mary Carlson*

Above: clean up at Misquamicut, Rhode Island.

Right: cottage damage in Misquamicut.

Opposite top: the Pleasant View Inn, Misquamicut.

Opposite bottom: Watch Hill, Rhode Island.

— *all photographs by Edward & Mary Carlson*

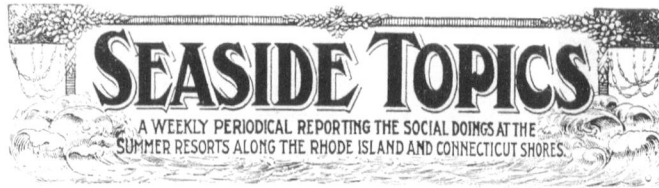

SEASIDE TOPICS

A WEEKLY PERIODICAL REPORTING THE SOCIAL DOINGS AT THE SUMMER RESORTS ALONG THE RHODE ISLAND AND CONNECTICUT SHORES

VOL. XXXV   SPECIAL HURRICANE ISSUE, NOVEMBER, 1938   PRICE ONE DOLLAR

Watch Hill Taken Unawares By Hurricane Meets a Major Disaster With Fortitude

The Hurricane of September 21st, 1938, was the severest and most destructive storm that has visited New England in recorded times. The vice chairman of the Red Cross, James L. Fieser, who has had charge of relief in every major disaster since 1913, reported: "I have never seen a hurricane more complete in its devastation. I cannot recall any instances where whole communities were blown away and left a pile of splintered wreckage more than a mile from their original sites." Comparing it with Florida hurricanes, Howard C. Babcock, of Orlando, Fla., who had a summer home at Misquamicut, declared that in 27 years' residence in that state during which he weathered all the hurricanes, he had experienced nothing to compare with the conditions in Westerly.

The tragedy of this hurricane was the total unawareness of this section to any such danger. Nobody at Watch Hill could conceive of anything worse than the annual "line storm" which always brought many out to watch the big breakers. There had been nothing like a hurricane since the "Great September Gale of 1815," of which many had read but never expected to see its like. Napatree Point was reported to have been heavily wooded before that storm.

Tropical hurricanes usually strike out into the North Atlantic after sweeping up past Cape Hatteras.

Starting in the doldrums near the Equator between South America and Africa they occur only from June to November and are most frequent in September. In the inside back cover of this booklet is the Weather Bureau's map showing the origin and course of this hurricane and the lines of barometric pressure which spelled a trough of least resistance through which it rushed with increasing velocity. Hurricane warnings had been issued by the Weather Bureau and ships at sea were enabled to get into harbor so that the Bureau had no reports from them to show that the storm was changing the customary course and was rushing on to the heavily populated and built up shores of Long Island and New England. It struck before anybody was aware that it was a hurricane. Then it was too late for those who lived in beach cottages to escape.

Watch Hill on that fateful Wednesday was totally oblivious to danger. Its shops were open and many cottages still occupied by those who love to stay on into the Fall. The morning had been mild and hazy with a brisk breeze blowing. Many went bathing as usual and remarked how warm the water was.

Mrs. John McKesson Camp was hostess at a luncheon on the rocks at Weekapaug and her guests gathered about one o'clock and only noticed that the sea looked restless and spoke of a strange yellow light over it. In the party were Mr. and Mrs. Nelson E. Perin, their two daughters, Mrs. Edward Burling, Jr., and Miss Anne Perin, Mrs. Frank A. Sayles, Mrs. Murray Cobb, Mrs. Harry Parsons Cross, and her sister, Mrs. Nathan C. Wyeth, Miss Elizabeth and Mr. Gregory Camp. Rising wind and rain broke up the party at about 2:30 and the return to the Hill found trees falling across the road. Mrs. Cobb, unable to get to her house, remained with the Perins.

Mrs. George Valentine Smith had left the Hill for Philadelphia on the Colonial, one of the last trains to get through on the New Haven Railroad for eighteen days. . . Mr. and Mrs. Daniel F. Larkin had a party out in their schooner, "Blue Sea.". . . Mrs. Vachel Anderson was at the Clifford Shinkle's when the storm came up and was unable to return to her cottage. . . .

"Bob" Loomis, last summer's popular Fort Road officer, was out in the open all through the storm and saw all that one could see through the flying spray and rain. He was mowing the lawn at his cottage on Larkin Road about 2 P. M. The wind got so wild that he went to the Coast Guard Station and asked the man in the tower what kind of a storm was expected. The guard said the barometer had been falling and it looked as if it might be bad. Loomis noticed an unusual pressure in his ears. The wind and rain were now blowing with such force that he made his way back behind the seawall toward the Rodman Griscom cottage—just in time to see its sun porch windows break and the

Above: excerpt from article from *Seaside Topics*.

Opposite: Atlantic Avenue in Misquamicut, Rhode Island before and after the storm. Both photographs were taken in front of the Pleasant View Inn.
— from "The Hurricane, September 21, 1938, Westerly, Rhode Island and Vicinity, Historical and Pictorial" by Lewis R. Greene

Franklin Square, Norwich, Conn. — *photograph from the collection of Robert Rousseau*

"YOU'RE NOT GOING TO BELIEVE THIS, BUT IT'S TRUE."

— Winthrop Benjamin

The stories in this book were collected seventy-five years after the Hurricane of 1938 barreled up the coast of New England. You may wonder how accurate these memories can be after so much time has passed. Some of the people interviewed were just four or five years old when the storm hit. You may think they were too young to remember anything clearly at all, let alone the details they reported.

The following is reprinted from a booklet titled *Hurricane Views–September 21, 1938*. It is an account of the storm written shortly after the hurricane by Myles Standish, a reporter from the Norwich Bulletin. It provides detailed proof of the power of memory, particularly when recalling an event as powerful as this storm.

Peaceful Eastern Connecticut, for generations smug in its belief that Nature, when on rampage, would never wreak destruction along the valleys of the Thames, the Shetucket and the Quinebaug, today looks askance at every breeze and rising tide. Residents of this corner of the Nutmeg state had, from time immemorial, felt secure from the hurricanes and floods of which they had read in other and far distant parts…

Almost over night this confidence was shattered, when on Wednesday, September 21, 1938, just as summer was turning into autumn, this section of Connecticut was visited by floods that inundated the lowlands to unprecedented depths; a hurricane that left a tangled waste of torn trees, power lines, and homes; and last, a tidal wave that swept beaches clean of cottages as though some mighty hand had wielded a gigantic broom, all combining to leave in their wake a record of destruction and death, never before experienced…

Starting with showers on September 14, which were intermittent until Saturday, the 17th, the rain came in torrential proportions for four days to completely saturate the ground to a point where it could hold no more. Rivers to the north of Norwich began as early as Sunday to rise slowly, and by Monday night had reached alarming proportions. Flood warnings were issued early Tuesday, the 20th, and by nightfall rivers were overflowing their banks. During the night, reports came in that dams were beginning to go out and that the water was fast approaching the flood stage of 1936. The dam at Stafford was the first to let go, tumbling a great force of water into the Willimantic River that hurtled down on the city of Willimantic, inundating that place to depths never before recorded. Every small stream was contributing plenty of water to the ever-rising flood. The Quinebaug reached flood tide during the night, as did the Shetucket and Yantic, all of which pour their waters into the Thames River at Norwich.

In Norwich anxious eyes kept careful watch on the rising tide which mounted inch by inch during the early morning hours of Wednesday. At mid-morning, the water was slowly creeping up toward the high water mark of 1936 and merchants in the vicinity of Franklin Square began frantically to remove stock from basements to the first floors where water had never reached before. At 2 o'clock the water was almost lapping at the very edges of Franklin Square and was rapidly rising.

Shortly before 3 o'clock there was a sudden rise in the water and those along the harbor front began to realize that a stiff wind was pushing the water back up the river. Not, even then did they realize that it was being hurled inland by the hurricane that at that particular time was some miles off the coast. Hurricane warnings had been broadcast from radio stations, coast guard stations were flying hurricane warning flags, but even then no one paid much attention. It couldn't happen here—hurricanes were a part of Florida's climate, not Connecticut's.

And then, blasting out of the southeast at a speed that at times reached 100 miles an hour came the hurricane. It was not one of the narrow twisters of a few yards width that sweep a path across the plains of the west, but a wide- spread affair that extended from New York to Nantucket, and the center seemed to sweep right up the Thames River over Norwich and on up the valleys in Eastern Connecticut until it spent itself far up in New Hampshire. The most notable feature was that the hurricane lasted almost two hours, then gradually abating, until toward midnight the skies were clear

and the stars looked down on destruction that was almost beyond comprehension.

Norwich first felt the force of the wind shortly before 3 o'clock when branches from trees began to fall and put out of commission power lines in various sections of the city. By 3 o'clock there was a growing feeling of apprehension, but even then no one had the slightest inkling that the wind would reach the proportions that it did. Perhaps the only ones who sensed the severity of the storm were the engineers at the Gas & Electric plant, who realized that the electricity in the city should be turned off to prevent any chance of fire resulting from fallen wires. The power went off completely at 3:20 o'clock, leaving mills, homes, and business houses without light.

…In less than 20 minutes after the hurricane hit Norwich, the city was completely cut off from the outside world, its streets choked with fallen trees, roofs of houses, frail garages, telephone, and light poles.

The business section of the city, around Franklin Square, and the streets along the harbor were awash with water, augmented by that rushing down from the Shetucket and Yantic Rivers. But the height of the flood was not yet—that coming with the darkness, between 8 and 9 o'clock. The water rose at a rate estimated at seven feet per hour between 5:30 and 7 o'clock.

While Norwich had experienced high water before, although not of such proportions, the real terror that drove, people to basements and cellars came during the height of the hurricane. With trees falling and roofs and walls of buildings toppling into streets, it is small wonder that more people were not injured or even killed. Norwich was indeed fortunate that there were no fatalities, there being only one death directly attributed to the storm, ... a woman suffered a shock brought on by the excitement of the hurricane.

As early as 3 o'clock in the afternoon the high wind was getting in its work of destruction, for to the south of the city reports of trees crashing into houses and across highways came into The Bulletin office before all telephone communication was cut off. However, the real force of the, storm was not felt in the city proper until about 3:30 when roofs of buildings started to peel off under the power of the wind. One of the first things to take the count was the town clock, whose four faces were blown completely out. Then the north tower of the United Congregational Church came crashing to earth, to be followed a few seconds later by the roof and front part of the top story of the Broadway School. The freight shed of the New Haven Railroad at the foot of Market and Shetucket Streets, weakened by the undermining effect of the water, could not withstand the terrific force of the wind and just crumbled where it stood. Around Franklin Square, where the buildings were forced to take the full brunt of the wind as it swept up the river, many of the landmarks

were wrecked, The top story of the Steiner Building on Main Street came hurtling to the street, the roof of the Columbian House went sailing off in company with the roofs of the Chelsea Lunch and the Somers Buildings. These roofs hit the Corey Building and the Tongren Building on Bath Street, toppling them into the street, total ruins. On the West Side, the Pearl Street school lost its belfry and roof as did the Riverside Home. At the International Silver Co. in Thamesville one wall crashed in after part of the roof had been carried away along with ventilators and chimneys. The Falls Mill suffered a quarter of million dollars in damage when almost the entire top story and roof was carried away, leaving the spooling room completely exposed to the storm. Smaller buildings belonging to the mill were unroofed and walls battered down...

Continuing northward up the Shetucket, Yantic, and Quinebaug Rivers, the hurricane wrought its havoc in all the mill villages along the streams... Sweeping up the Shetucket River valley, the hurricane crashed in the glass and steel roof of the J. B. Martin Co., blew off a corner of Sacred Heart Church at Taftville, and laid waste to the beautiful stand of fir trees in front of the Ponemah Mills. The Ponemah Mills withstood the hurricane very well losing only small sections of roofing, but the water took a heavy toll. When the east part of the Ponemah dam washed out, it undermined the ell of the mill at the north end and part of this toppled into the river...

Along the Quinebaug the fury of the hurricane was also felt. At Jewett City all three of the mills, the Aspinook Company, the Ashland Cotton Co., and the Jewett City Textile Novelty Co., suffered heavily. The roofs of the Aspinook and the Ashland were torn apart while at the Novelty Co. the entire back part of the mill was blown in, part of which included a new addition... Some inkling of the terrific force of the hurricane can be gained by evidence at Wauregan, where the Chabot farm barn, containing 300 tons of hay was literally lifted from its foundation and then dropped in the highway 30 feet away, barn, hay and all...

The hurricane was bad, but the worst was yet to follow, especially along the coast towns, seashore resorts, and in Norwich. Following on the heels of the hurricane came a devastating tidal wave dragged in by the suction caused by the terrific wind and this took an appalling toll in lives, shipping, and summer cottages. However, it was not until the next day that the extent of the damage began to filter through to Norwich, which for 12 hours was as isolated from the rest of the world as if it had been on some distant planet.

Norwich, from all observations of those who have traveled the stricken area from end to end, was the hardest hit place in Eastern Connecticut, and the property loss reached well into the millions and is steadily mounting, even after weeks of clean-up work, as new damage is discovered.

When the force of the hurricane had spent itself around 5 o'clock in the afternoon and people dared venture into the streets of the downtown section, they were sent scurrying back to their places of business by the surprising and alarming rise in the water. Not knowing of the tidal wave that had hit the coast, they were at a loss to account for it, but they worked frantically to rescue merchandise from ground floors where they had thought it to be safe, as all other periods of high water had never touched it.

With water rising at the rate of seven feet per hour, they could do little other than save a few hundred dollars worth of stock. The water came swirling across the docks along the harbor, up Rose Place into Franklin Square, bearing with it floating timbers from wrecked factories and other buildings, motor boats, and other debris which crashed into windows and buildings and did additional damage to already badly damaged buildings. Within the short space of three hours after the passing of the hurricane the downtown business section of the city was literally afloat. People marooned in buildings were driven to second stories where they huddled in a darkness made more fearsome because of the gurgling of the water beneath them... Those caught around the area that embraces Franklin

Square just had to stay in the building or swim for it.

At the corner of Franklin and Bath Streets, by actual measurement, the water was eight feet and one inch deep, while along the Shetucket Street docks, through lower Market and Commerce Streets it was slightly higher. Its height exceeded the past record, set by the flood of 1886 by some six feet. This was especially evident on the railroad trestle over the Shetucket River, where the water was 70 inches *over* the railroad tracks … In Rose Place, in front of the Palace Theatre, the high water washed just under the marquee, making a depth at this point, which is lower than Franklin Square, of about 11 feet.

…The dams at Occum, Taftville, Danielson, Stafford Springs, and Mansfield all went out and bridges at Occum and Baltic were swept away, as were smaller bridges over brooks along the highways. Dyer dam at Danielson was the last to go out, breaking up in the early morning hours of Thursday. The Eighth Street bridge in the Greeneville section of Norwich was swept away during Wednesday night and parts of it were found days later about 500 yards north of the drawbridge in New London, 13 miles away…

Early in the evening of the disaster, military, police, and relief organizations started to function. Shortly after the height of the hurricane had been reached, the militia was called out to aid the police in warning people from the flooded sections of the city. Streets were roped off and patrolled but it was not until late in the evening that strict regulations were laid down. Norwich was not under strict martial law, but rather under a semi-martial law condition, with the military cooperating with the civic authorities to maintain order and prevent looting, of which there was very little and of no consequence. By midnight it was necessary to get passes to enter restricted areas. This condition continued for approximately ten days, (until) Sunday night, October 8…

Early Wednesday evening the Red Cross, which had been called out, started to really function in its work of relief… the Red Cross set up headquarters in the S. N. E. Telephone office on Broadway, and relief work went on with surprising smoothness. The American Legion, Boy Scouts, Girl Scouts, and Naval Reserves also lent aid in this work and did a mighty fine job.

Health authorities of the city swung into action, calling on local physicians to assist, as well as bringing in the state health authorities. Stringent health regulations were laid down and inoculations against typhoid were started and thousands were given the inoculations over a period of a few hours. The result is self-evident, as there has not been a single ease of the disease in the city that can be attributed to the flood. The State Health Department, with a corps of workers, started its work of directing the clean-up. Merchandise and equipment

Franklin Street in Norwich, Conn. the day after the storm. — *photograph by Edward & Mary Carlson*

damaged by the flood were ordered thrown away, and in a short space of time, considering the magnitude of the disaster, the health situation was well in hand.

Following close on the heels of the health authorities came the federal aid in the form of the W. P. A., the N. Y. A., Coast Guard, and the boys from the CCC camps to the number of several hundreds. These men did efficient work in cleaning up the city of flood debris, opening tree-choked streets and rushing along the work of rehabilitation…

What is true of the utilities is true all through the area. Damage is being repaired at all possible speed, but it will be a long time before everything is back to normal again and some of it never will be. Many buildings in Norwich have been condemned and must be torn down and rebuilt. Trees, stately and beautiful, have gone, and it will be years upon years before Norwich ever approaches its former verdant beauty.

As has been said, Norwich suffered no loss of lives, but this cannot be said of the communities along the shore. It was here that the great loss of life took place and very few shore resorts escaped with no one being drowned or crushed under broken cottages. Misquamicut, on the Rhode Island shore, along with Atlantic Beach and Watch Hill, suffered the largest death toll. There have been nearly 300 known deaths. The tidal wave that hit the coast just swept the beaches clean, piled up debris a mile from the shore front, drove big fishing and pleasure craft to places far from the waters edge. Other craft, just sank at the moorings, while others went drifting out to sea when the wave receded and may never be seen again.

Stonington, historical seaport town, took a bad water-front beating, as did Mystic, Lord's Point and Groton Long Point, where cottages were torn apart, blown or washed from foundations and not more than one per cent escaped without some damage.

At New London shipping piled up on the waterfront in a grotesque mass. A big ship rode onto railroad tracks high above the water; others broke loose and driven and buffeted by wind and water, wrought havoc among smaller craft and the piers. New London was most unfortunate in that a fire started along the waterfront at the height of the hurricane and before it could be brought under control it had swept through three city blocks along Bank Street doing damage that amounted to well over $2,000,000. Ocean Beach was practically wiped out and the beaches to the west Pleasure Beach, Crescent Beach, Saybrook and others also took their beatings to a more or less degree…

Today Eastern Connecticut is struggling back and despite the severity of the setback, the rugged New England spirit of these, our people, will carry them on to a more determined effort to make Eastern Connecticut a place of which to be proud.

With appreciation to everyone who shared their stories of the storm.

www.ingramcontent.com/pod-product-compliance
Lightning Source LLC
Chambersburg PA
CBHW061053090426
42742CB00002B/28